The Meter and Melody of *Beowulf*

The Meter and Melody of *Beowulf*

Thomas Cable

ILLINOIS STUDIES IN
LANGUAGE AND LITERATURE
64

UNIVERSITY OF ILLINOIS PRESS
Urbana Chicago London
1974

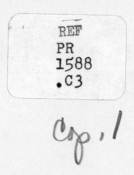

Printed in Great Britain
by William Clowes & Sons, Limited, London, Beccles and Colchester
Library of Congress Catalog Card No. 72–97683
ISBN 0–252–00348–9

To my mother and the memory of my father

Acknowledgments

The published works that this study is most indebted to will become clear soon enough—especially works by Eduard Sievers, John C. Pope, A. J. Bliss, W. K. Wimsatt, Jr., and Winfred P. Lehmann. In a less obvious way, the study owes something to a spirit of optimism and confidence that prevailed in American linguistics during the middle and late 1960's. It was during this period that I sketched the outlines, gathered the evidence, and submitted to the Graduate School of the University of Texas the doctoral dissertation that was the original form of the present argument. It would not be surprising if, in its final form, the argument retains some of the strengths and weaknesses of linguistic inquiry during that stimulating period.

On a more personal level, I am indebted to criticism by James Sledd, whose relentless brass tacks punctured much that was puncturable, early and late. I have also had the considerable benefit of long discussions and correspondence about Old English meter with Ruth P. Lehmann. For reading the manuscript at various stages and making detailed comments, I owe thanks to four medievalists, M. M. Crow, Jackson J. Campbell, Joseph B. Trahern, Jr., and James W. Marchand. For similar help, and for assuring me that I was at least asking the right questions, I am indebted to Emmon Bach and Winfred P. Lehmann.

The program of Summer Faculty Fellowships at the University of Illinois made it possible for me to devote two full summers to expanding and revising the original draft. During this time I also had an opportunity to test parts of the theory in print. For permission to include those parts that have already been published, I wish to thank the editors of three journals. The substance of Chapter Three appeared in *Modern Philology*, 69 (1971), 97–104; of Chapter Four in *Neuphilologische Mitteilungen*, 72 (1971), 42–50; and of Chapter Six in *Studies in Philology*, 69 (1972), 280–88.

The editors of Illinois Studies in Language and Literature have been most helpful, understanding, and patient in dealing with a typographically difficult manuscript. In particular, I would like to express my appreciation to Allan Holaday, Chairman of the Board of Editors, and to Richard L. Wentworth, Associate Director and Editor of the University of Illinois Press.

Finally, I owe a hopeless debt to my wife Carole, who has seen too many drafts of this already and who no doubt will be greatly relieved to get Cædmon's ghost out of the house.

Austin, Texas   T. C.
November 1972

Contents

Introduction

Some of the goals of the chapters that follow are more modest than others. The more modest goals have to do with the drier aspects of the rather dry matter of meter, and for that they evoke apology. The less modest goals are cause for apology also, for they put one in the position of possibly claiming too much. Inflated claims are less easily recognized than mere tedium, and harder to avoid, but more serious. Two works on Old English versification that have recently appeared in second editions, by John C. Pope and A. J. Bliss,[1] make large claims supported by imposing arguments. Pope believes that his discovery "has proved of amazing efficacy in producing the metrical order and expressiveness which we associate with competent poetry"; it is the "vital clue" that makes Germanic poetry something other than "a very queer and unintelligible thing" (pp. 3–4). Bliss, in the preface to his first edition, purports to offer "a triumphant vindication of Sievers," and "a number of interesting discoveries which, once discovered, seemed so obvious that it was difficult to understand how they had been overlooked so long" (p. v).

If an investigator makes what he considers to be discoveries, as Bliss and Pope do, there is nothing to do but call them that and take the risk of having them shown to be something else; otherwise, he misrepresents his own work by representing it too lightly. If he considers his work original enough to amount to a theory, as Pope does, he should call it such and take the risk of having it shown to be trivial or false. In the relatively tedious part of the present study, Chapters Two through Six, I present a number of small discoveries. For the most part, these discoveries support or refine the theory of meter devised by Eduard Sievers, the theory from which all other theories must begin.[2] Then, in Chapter Seven, I present a considerably larger discovery that rests directly upon each of the chapters preceding it, and which might be called a theory: there I argue that the Five Types of Old English verse are the logical result of a single principle. Four types, or six, or three, would be arbitrary, but five types are exactly the number to expect from the single principle if the principle is interpreted through the constraints explained in Chapters Two through Six. Finally, in Chapter Eight I attempt to relate the abstract pattern of Chapter Seven to matters of more general interest: on the one hand, to linguistic prosody, especially pitch, and on the other to music—Gregorian and Byzantine chant, *chansons de geste*, oral-formulaic theory, the lyre. The inexpert application that I make of my abstract pattern I would hesitate to call either discovery or theory; in Jess Bessinger's phrase, I undertake but to hypothesize inoffensively.[3] However, I would defend with some tenacity the abstract pattern upon which the hypotheses rest.

My apology, in short, amounts to this: I see the present study as making a series of progressively larger claims. The argument for the metrical relevance of secondary stress, the subject of Chapter Four, is a relatively cautious argument in support of a relatively modest claim. So are the arguments and claims of Chapter Two, which denies the existence of "light verses"; of Chapter Three, which adduces certain syntactic constraints upon anacrusis; of Chapter Five, which asserts that the first of two clashing stresses is always heavier; and of Chapter Six, which reclassifies several categories of Sievers' type D. These chapters are frankly technical and will primarily interest the specialist in Old English prosody. The less specialized reader may find more profit in Chapter One, which reviews certain ideas that appear in prominent theories and repeatedly in the handbooks; Chapter Seven, which summarizes and synthesizes as a theory the preceding technical discussions; and Chapter Eight, which uses that theory to present a number of new reasons for believing that the older verse was sung—and to reconstruct some possible melodies.

Most of this book consists of traditional metrical analysis, the kind of analysis to be found in works by Sievers, Kaluza, Heusler, Pope, and Bliss. From these works I take individual metrical patterns, posit the patterns as expressions of metrical reality, and proceed to consider the implications. Sievers' Five Types of Germanic verse were based on a statistical survey of existing texts; for *Beowulf*, Bliss has supported and expanded upon Sievers' discoveries by developing the statistical method in some detail. This kind of tabulation and refinement is indeed one of the implications to draw from a posited pattern. But in addition to tabulating the patterns that occur, one is obliged to consider the patterns that do not, and to ask whether the theory plausibly accounts for their absence. To inquire about missing patterns is nearly as important as to describe existing ones.

Much of the argument of this book insists that such an inquiry has not been adequately pursued in descriptions of Old English meter—that the extensive catalogues of verses provided by Sievers, Bliss, and Pope contain no sufficient rule of exclusion, no constraint to prevent an extension of the catalogues to include other patterns. There are good reasons, syntactically and rhetorically, to expect patterns that in fact do not occur. If those patterns were systematically excluded by the meter, then a system which fails to reveal the principle of exclusion may well fail to state the meter at all. The classifications, indices, and catalogues that such a system inspires may be at once quite helpful and quite misleading.

One risks appearing ungrateful. Anyone who works with Old English meter must remain indebted to Pope and Bliss for the thoroughness, care, and accuracy of their compilations. Both scholars, however, include metatheoretical statements that may be taken as fair warning: any classification will assume certain features to be significant and others to be irrelevant, depending upon the underlying theory. If the theory is faulty, then the catalogues may mislead as much as they help.

The potential to mislead is especially clear when the essentials of a detailed theory are abstracted, summarized, and stated baldly. If one sees Sievers' system as a two-beat theory, in opposition to earlier four-beat theories, then one can make the sort of statement about Old English poetry that occurs repeatedly in the handbooks: that the meter is based ultimately upon two main stresses to the verse. I shall argue that such a statement not merely oversimplifies; it positively distorts. In order to explain basic inconsistencies in Sievers' theory, I have found it necessary to return to certain ideas set forth in nineteenth-century four-beat theories—in the work of pioneer investigators such as Karl Lachmann, E. Jessen, Arthur Amelung, Bernhard ten Brink, Moritz Trautmann, and Max Kaluza, work now largely ignored. Similarly, one may assert of Pope's theory, as Robert P. Creed does, that its main problem is its complexity. Taking an analogy from linguistics, Creed compares the full theory to a narrow phonetic transcription and proceeds to look for the rhythmical equivalent of phonemes.[4] But after all the complexity of Pope's system is stripped away, one must retain the pause, the silent ictus, the harp beat, in B and C verses if one retains the system at all. One must believe that two of the five metrical types consistently required a non-syllabic unit—this in order to have a measure as the measure is defined. One can then only conclude that the old Germanic poetry was quite unlike any other poetry or music, so far as I am aware, past or present. From Bliss's discoveries one may go even further and decide, as did Marjorie Daunt, that there is no meter at all, simply the cadences of prose.[5]

In the final chapter of this book, I try to step back from the details of my own analysis and ask simple questions. Perhaps the simplest should ultimately be asked of any such description: What kind of psychological and aesthetic reality could this quasi-mathematical system have had? In originally turning to acoustic and musical patterns, I was looking for an external kind of confirmation: the assurance that the sort of abstract pattern that I posit for Old English verse exists elsewhere, in theory or in history. The preliminary investigations beyond the narrow area of my competence have revealed certain relationships too striking to be dismissed as an amateur's fancy.

For acoustic matters, I have relied especially upon the work of

Philip Lieberman, Dwight Bolinger, D. B. Fry, and David Crystal. Their theories often overlap with musical theory, and for my purposes are most interesting when they do. A principle of poetic composition by melodic formula, such as Egon Wellesz describes for Byzantine chant and Paolo Ferretti for Gregorian, is more than a possibility for *Beowulf*. If a system of melodic formulas does indeed underlie the meter, it may well be more basic than the lexical and syntactic formulas that have been examined in so much scholarship since Francis P. Magoun, Jr., first applied oral-formulaic analysis to Old English verse. My own conclusions regarding the musical performance of Old English poetry are similar in certain respects to conclusions drawn in recent studies by Ewald Jammers and Dietrich Hofmann; in other respects, they support hypotheses concerning the use of the Old English harp, especially as described in work by Jess B. Bessinger, Jr., and by C. L. Wrenn.

The concern throughout this study is with the 6,342 normal verses in *Beowulf*. I shall have nothing to say about the twenty-two hypermetric verses.

NOTES

[1] John C. Pope, *The Rhythm of Beowulf*, 2nd ed. rev. (New Haven: Yale University Press, 1966), and A. J. Bliss, *The Metre of Beowulf*, 2nd ed. rev. (Oxford: Blackwell, 1967).

[2] See especially Eduard Sievers, "Zur Rhythmik des germanischen Alliterationsverses I," *Beiträge zur Geschichte der deutschen Sprache und Literatur*, 10 (1885), 209–314, and *Altgermanische Metrik* (Halle: Niemeyer, 1893).

[3] Jess B. Bessinger, Jr., "The Sutton Hoo Harp Replica and Old English Musical Verse," in *Old English Poetry: Fifteen Essays*, ed. Robert P. Creed (Providence, R.I.: Brown University Press, 1967), pp. 13–14. Bessinger's essay is a valuable introduction to the archeological and musicological problems of Old English poetry.

[4] Robert P. Creed, "A New Approach to the Rhythm of *Beowulf*," *PMLA*, 81 (1966), 23.

[5] Marjorie Daunt, "Old English Verse and English Speech Rhythm," *Transactions of the Philological Society* (1946), pp. 56–72.

ONE

Problems in Old English Prosody

Several years ago, in a fine essay on meter, W. K. Wimsatt, Jr., and Monroe C. Beardsley discussed two influential schools of scansion—the linguistic and the temporal—and faults that they believed to be basic to each.[1] The import of their criticism is of less interest for our discussion than is the framework that they discerned and used, for something like it may be borrowed to aid in the exposition of Old English prosody. While I am not wholly persuaded that the arguments by Wimsatt and Beardsley against the temporal view are the right arguments to make, I would like to follow their organization by turning, in the second half of this chapter, to a consideration of that view and of rhythmical theory. In place of Northrop Frye on Modern English poetry, we shall consider John C. Pope's theory of the rhythm of *Beowulf*.

The other point of departure for Wimsatt and Beardsley was the view of meter influenced by Trager-Smith phonology. "Linguistic" is suggestive but not quite adequate as a label to characterize this faulty view of the Old English verse-form. Linguists (now generative-transformationalists instead of structuralists) figure prominently in the fallacy that I have in mind, but it is a fallacy shared also by Wimsatt and Beardsley and stated without a hint of doubt in many handbooks. It holds that the essential statement to make about Old English meter (after noting the alliteration) is this: each verse, each half-line of poetry, contains two main stresses and an indeterminate number of weaker stresses. This view enjoys considerable authority, for it purports to summarize the classic system devised by Eduard Sievers. It implies that one could proceed to give the full complexity of his system—to talk about secondary stress and syllabic length and resolution and suspension of resolution and anacrusis—and all of this would simply make more precise and complete the statement of two main stresses to the verse. I shall argue that the simplified statement distorts Old English meter in a very serious way and that it does not even represent Sievers' system accurately.

The most important point that these chapters try to make is that Sievers' system *can* be simplified—dramatically—and still contain most of the elements originally included within it. Before proceeding to examine what I consider to be unsuccessful simplifications, it will help to sketch the outlines of the original system. By Sievers' view, a line of Old English poetry consists of two *verses* (also called *half-lines* or *hemistichs*), which consist in turn of two *feet*. A foot contains a long syllable bearing full stress (the *arsis*) and a varying number of syllables bearing secondary and weak stress (the *thesis*); secondary stress usually occurs on a long syllable, weak stress indifferently on a long or a short.[2] Sievers' five types of half-lines are familiar:

A	´ x | ´ x
B	x ´ | x ´
C	x ´ | ´ x
D1	´ | ´ ˋ x
D2	´ | ´ x ˋ
E	´ ˋ x | ´

The two half-lines are bound together by alliteration, which may occur in either or both arses of the first half-line (the a-verse) but only in the first arsis of the second half-line (the b-verse), where alliteration is obligatory. Other rules allow for resolved stress (whereby a short stressed syllable and the following syllable, long

$$´\,x$$

or short, are scanned as one: *wiga*) and suspension of resolution in certain contexts (usually in the penultimate syllable of the verse,

$$x$$

when that syllable follows a metrically stressed syllable: *þæt*

$$´\quad ˘\, x$$

healreced).[3] These basic principles, presented here in greatly abbreviated form, are explained concisely in the second chapter of *Altgermanische Metrik*.[4]

It does not help the cause of literary history to explain this rather complex system of meter by analogy with certain modern forms, or to draw the familiar distinction between old strong stress meter and newer accentual-syllabic meter. The distinction, a superficially helpful one, appears in textbook summaries of Old English prosody and in otherwise tough-minded discussions as introductory background to the prosody of Modern English. Wimsatt and Beardsley contrast Modern English iambic pentameter with the "very old (and recently revived) meter of strong stress" in terms that may be taken as fairly representative of the view which I oppose:

This other kind of meter is older in English poetry and may be more natural to the English tongue, though again it may not be. Here only the major stresses of the major words count in the scanning. The gabble of weaker syllables, now more, now fewer, between the major stresses obscures all the minor stresses and relieves them of any structural duty. . . . Thus we have *Beowulf*, *Piers Plowman*, *Everyman*, Spenser's *February Eclogue*, Coleridge's *Christabel*, the poetry of G. M. Hopkins . . . the poetry of T. S. Eliot, and many another in our day.[5]

Now it may be that something is to be gained from characterizing *Piers Plowman*, *Everyman*, the *February Eclogue*, *Christabel*, and the poetry of Hopkins and Eliot as poetry written in strong stress meter. I must confess uncertainty. What I am indeed certain of is that *Beowulf* should be promptly removed from the group.

Wimsatt and Beardsley take the opening lines of *Piers Plowman* to make their point, and the example is a familiar one. I would use the same lines, however, to make a contrary point, that the principle of two stresses to the half-line with weaker syllables clustered around them does not tell us what we need to know about Old English meter. The first line of *Piers Plowman* contains a pattern that occurs frequently in the Middle English poem, but not at all in *Beowulf*:[6]

x x ′ x ′ x
In a somer seson, whan soft was the sonne

It is no accident that x x ⏜ x ⏜ x is absent from *Beowulf*. The syntax of the words underlying the pattern is common in all periods of English, and there is every reason to expect the pattern to occur. It can be argued that the syntactically most probable of *all* two-stress patterns in Old English has unstressed syllables before and after the stresses.[7] Yet the meter of *Beowulf*, which contains by Bliss's count some 130 patterns such as x x x x x ⏜ x | x ⏜ and ⏜ | ⏜ : x ⏜ and other patterns still more exotic, does not employ the very ordinary pattern that begins *Piers Plowman*.

It is easy to miss the significance of a negative statement to the effect that a certain pattern does not occur, or occurs only once. One should bear in mind that there are some 6,364 verses in *Beowulf*; and one should consider the ease with which a poet writing in English, Old or Modern, could construct phrases of the pattern, *In a somer seson*—a syntactic pattern beginning with an unstressed preposition or article or conjunction, containing two main stresses on adjective and noun, and ending on an unstressed inflectional or derivational syllable. And one should consider the view of Old English meter that prescribes two main stresses and an indeterminate number of weaker stresses. One can then reasonably ask why the expected patterns do not occur—why, among the 6,364 verses, there are not several hundred or a thousand verses like the one that begins *Piers Plowman*. J. P. Oakden notes that the type of verse which he calls *Rising-Falling-Rhythm* (type A with one or more syllables of anacrusis) is the most frequently used of all patterns in Middle English.[8] Syntactically, its frequency is understandable. And it would have been the most frequently used pattern in Old English except that the meter then was significantly different: the meter specifically excluded the type of pattern that would have been the easiest and most natural to construct. The mechanism of exclusion is what the traditional view of strong stress meter, with its freely occurring weaker syllables, fails to recognize.

Similarly, Northrop Frye's scansion of iambic pentameter lines as four-stress meter is generally accepted as Old English meter imposed (for better or for worse) upon the Modern English meter.[9] The first line of Hamlet's soliloquy, by Frye's view, might be read as a line of Old English:

To be, or not to be: that is the question

Note well that even those who disagree that the four-stress meter is there, believe that if it *were*, the meter would be suitable for *Beowulf*.[10] But the pattern of the first phrase, x $\perp$ x $\perp$ x x, occurs not at all in *Beowulf*, and again I would argue that the absence is not fortuitous but a result of a system of meter quite contrary to the system traditionally described in the handbooks. The conclusion that I draw is that one cannot hold as a general principle that the poet attended only to two stresses to the half-line and let the more weakly stressed syllables take care of themselves.

A recognizable variant of the fallacy in question occurs in theories that require only a single stress instead of two. Among the subtypes of the five main types are verses that A. J. Bliss reads with only one metrical stress and calls "light verses";[11] he catalogues twelve light patterns of type A, such as 762a and 1877a:

a1c
762a   Mynte se mǣra,   (þ)ǣr hē meahte swā

a2d
1877a   þæt hē þone brēostwylm   forberan ne mehte

The question of whether Bliss's light patterns are valid for Old English is an important and technical one that must be saved for full discussion in Chapter Two. Here it is sufficient to note the process of classification and the elements considered to be metrically relevant. In addition to stressed, unstressed, and secondarily stressed syllables, Bliss pays close attention to what he calls the caesura. Type A has forty-three different shapes by his count, of which the following are representative:

1A1a(i) $\perp$ | x $\perp$ x
1A*1b $\perp$ x | x x $\perp$ x
2A3b $\perp$ $\perp$ | $\breve{\,}$ x

The kind of caesura that occurs in these patterns is nothing like the feature by the same name that occurs in the poetry of Alexander Pope. An appropriate definition for Bliss's entity would be something like the following: a caesura is the first word boundary following a metrically stressed syllable. But if a caesura is simply a word boundary, we have in hand a linguistic concept, an element of the syntactic structure, and not necessarily an element of meter.

One can ask whether the linguistic concept of word boundary is a meaningful abstraction for meter—a question not rhetorical, for some scholars would answer it in the affirmative, including Marjorie Daunt, who puts forth as a "revolutionary suggestion" the idea that there was no meter in Old English apart from purely linguistic elements: "All the previous commentators have made (often unconsciously) a fundamental assumption, namely, that in Old English poetry we are dealing with a 'poetic metre', a definite artistic medium which needed to be acquired, of the same nature as later verse forms, though quite different in shape."[12] From passages of Old English prose, a letter by Lord Oxford, and an advertisement in the *Evening News*, Miss Daunt concludes that Old English verse "is really the spoken language rather tidied up."[13]

This view of poetry as prose derives ultimately, at least in part, from the view that perceives the "gabble of weaker syllables" falling as they may; and it suffers the same problems. If the patterns of meter are simply a set of selected linguistic patterns, by what principle can one explain the basis of selection? Why should just those patterns occur that do occur, and why should other patterns, which there is every reason syntactically to expect, fail to occur? Bliss gives us an exhaustive list of syllabic patterns in *Beowulf*, but he gives no general qualifications for the list, no principles that reveal what the metrical patterns have in common. Other patterns could be added, including those which Bliss would consider unmetrical, and there would be no logical basis for excluding them.

I am by no means the first to object to lists of patterns as a statement of the meter. S. J. Keyser has lodged a similar objection to such lists, phrased in arguments and terminology borrowed from generative grammar.[14] Instead of expanding Sievers' system as Bliss has done, Keyser tries to simplify it in order to find what the various patterns have in common. Though his simple system is able to describe all of the verses of *Beowulf*, it is also flexible enough to describe much more than that, including patterns that could hardly be considered metrical. James Sledd makes an important comment upon Keyser's theory when he says that "it is altogether *too* accommodating" and offers the following nonsense lines as extremes of the extraordinary range of patterns that the theory would admit:

bāt bāt   bātes
caldum clommum caldum clommum   caldum clommum caldum
                                                                                    clommum[15]

Keyser gains this flexibility of metrical description partly by abandoning Sievers' analysis of three features and offering alternative analyses of his own. Specifically, he argues against the metrical significance of secondary stress, the metrical significance of syllabic length, and the necessity of at least four syllables to the half-line. In each case I believe that Sievers' original system is superior to Keyser's refinement, but since the details are rather involved, I must refer to my treatment of them below.[16] In terms of the present discussion, Keyser's theory allows so much freedom in the placing of weaker syllables that poetry becomes no different from prose.

We must turn now to rhythmical theories and first of all understand that they deal with the same problems that concern the theories already discussed—a fact that is often obscured by both sides. Opponents and supporters of the rhythmical view tend to see two different domains, one of meter and one of rhythm, and to assume that a theory such as Sievers' could accommodate a theory such as Pope's, or vice versa. Pope, for example, says of Bliss's *The Metre of Beowulf*: "As the title implies, the author's main interest is not rhythm. . . . In his general aim, however, and in many of his conclusions there is no necessary conflict with my theory, and although I have not tried to adjust my interpretation to his in a thorough fashion, I have adopted a few of his readings

later in this preface."[17] And Keyser, in following Sievers' theory,
dismisses Pope's as one of performance: "It may well be that
Pope's conception of how *Beowulf* is to be performed corresponded
to the Old English bard's conception, though how this correspondence is to be recovered is difficult to see. At any rate, Pope's belief
that it is in error to hold to 'the notion that rhythm can exist
without strict temporal relations' is itself based upon a confusion
of rhythm and meter. Pope's comment is certainly true of rhythm,
but quite irrelevant with respect to meter, and it was the latter
which Sievers was attempting to characterize."[18] With a trace of
condescension, each scholar views the other's work as having aims
different from his own, and thereby dismisses it.

The point to make, of course, is that the aims of the two types
of theories are not different but quite the same. Sievers, Bliss, and
Keyser on the one hand—Heusler, Pope, and Creed on the other—
all attempt to discover and make explicit the principles that give
order and regularity to the older verse-form. In this attempt, both
types of theories deal with an abstract, idealized pattern; neither
tries to record the accidental features and idiosyncrasies of an
individual performance. In taking an analogy from linguistics,
where the concepts of *performance* and *competence* have technical
meanings, Keyser makes clear his understanding of a theory such
as Pope's. I would argue, however, that the analogy is misapplied
and that it should be used to make the opposite point. Pope's
system qualifies as a system of meter by the very criteria that
Keyser lays down, for it is "the specification, first, of a set of
abstract patterns which comprise the meter of a poem and second,
a set of rules which specify whether an arbitrary sequence of a
language qualifies as a realization of that meter."[19] Pope lists the
279 abstract patterns that he believes comprise the meter of the
poem—patterns such as C21:

$$(\prime)\backprime \quad \prime\prime \backslash\backslash$$
$$| \, \natural \, \rfloor \; | \; \rfloor \, \rfloor\!\!\_\rfloor \; |$$

And he gives a set of "realization rules" to translate the abstract
pattern into a sequence of syllables—rules that state the various crotchets, quavers, accents, ligatures, and rests in terms of

linguistic elements such as word stress, syllabic length, pause, and the like.[20] With Pope's two sets of rules, one can characterize any sequence of Old English as metrical or not. Verse 285a, *on hēahstede*, which is a realization of the pattern above, is admitted as metrical; and verse 2150a, *lissa gelong*, which does not fit any of Pope's permissible patterns, is catalogued as deficient—as are three other verses in the first half-line and two in the second. In this respect, his system is like Sievers', Bliss's, and even Keyser's.

Pope gives us his version of a particular performance, on a record produced by Educational Audio Visual,[21] and it is interesting to note that in places his performance fails to match the idealized norm. Such is the nature of a performance; but the score of his symphony is written with mathematical precision throughout some two hundred pages of *The Rhythm of Beowulf*. Note again Keyser's misapplication of a familiar analogy from linguistics: "Thus the relationship of a poem's meter to its performance is quite like that of the score of a symphony to its performance. The musical score remains quite unaffected by the performance" (p. 351). Presumably because of the use of measures and initial rests, Keyser relegates Pope's theory to the world of performance. The obvious comment to make is that the score of a symphony contains measures and rests as part of the abstract pattern; and if the measures and rests are misplaced in the score, a given line of music can be characterized as unacceptable—with nothing at all said about the performance. It is conceivable that the verse-form of *Beowulf*, like the score of the *Ninth*, requires measures and rests as a part of the abstract pattern. Keyser assumes otherwise—that only certain linguistic units, *syllable*, *word boundary*, *stress*, count in the meter. But his assumption is only that: an assumption (which ignores even syllabic length), and his metatheoretical comments about Pope's system follow deductively from the axioms that he asserts or implies.

This takes us to the main problem in Pope's system. Whereas Keyser assumes that equal measures cannot be a part of the meter, Pope assumes at the outset that they *must* be. What appears to be a carefully constructed argument is simply an unfolding of consequences that are plausible enough if one accepts the initial premises.

The premises are based upon the way Pope himself prefers to read the verse. It need hardly be pointed out that other expert readers have preferred different interpretations, or even that a careful listener may hear, in Pope's reading, patterns significantly different from those that he prescribes.[22] The key words in his argument are "assumption," "belief," "opinion": "the assumption that the normal half-line or verse contains two measures of quadruple time";[23] his "belief, founded on experimental readings, that the rhythmic basis of every normal verse, whether on-verse or off-verse, is a pair of dipodies, or four-beat measures."[24] Robert P. Creed follows Pope by beginning where Pope begins, with "the assumption that the *measure*, not the verse, provides the most significant clue to the simplicity of Old English prosody."[25] It is this assumption that precludes Pope's consideration of alternative proposals: "Isochrony and initial rests are so vital, in my opinion, for the achievement of an adequate sense of order in opposition to the extraordinary variety of syllabic patterns in the verses that I cannot take seriously certain counterproposals, made since 1942, which reject one or both of these features."[26]

The assumption of two measures to the verse in Old English, far from being self-evident, is historically implausible; but more of this below. It is conjoined with a second assumption that is not merely implausible, but false: that temporally equal measures of poetry and music can be perceived only if there is a recurring accent. In Pope's theory, the first accent of types A, D, and E occurs on a stressed syllable; in types B and C, the first accent usually falls on a pause, filled by a stroke of the harp:

42a   on flōdes æht   feor gewītan

B1

R. B. Le Page has correctly characterized as dogma the assertion that a measure must begin with an accent.[27] For an excellent discussion of the complex psychological problems involved in the perception of beats and of equal measures, one may consult Grosvenor W. Cooper and Leonard B. Meyer, *The Rhythmic Structure of Music* (Chicago: University of Chicago Press, 1960), pp. 1–11, et passim. For an understanding of the historical implausibility of a system predicated upon the twin assumptions of measures and recurring beats, one may consult any of the handbooks on music history. Gustave Reese writes:

The conception of "measure" has changed through the ages. In the music most frequently performed today, i.e. that of the 18th and 19th centuries, a measure consists of a pattern of beats, of which the first is accented, and the pattern recurs over and over. In 20th-century music the feature of recurrence is no longer essential: a composer like Stravinsky may sometimes change his time-signature in almost every measure. Fifteenth- and 16th-century polyphony, on the other hand, is an example of music in which the initial accent is the unessential feature: the stress may occur at the beginning of a measure but it does not have to.[28]

Pope has imposed a modern conception of rhythm, derived from familiar music of the eighteenth and nineteenth centuries, upon eighth-century poetry.

At least three critics of Pope's system have pointed out that the only contemporary music of which we have detailed knowledge, Gregorian chant, has nothing like the isochronous measures that Pope describes.[29] These observations Pope dismisses out of hand: "There would seem to be no likelihood that Old English verse, with its roots deep in the Germanic past, had at any time experienced the influence of a type of music devised in the Mediterranean world for the chanting of liturgical prose."[30] The point, of course, is not that Gregorian chant influenced Old English poetry (though in eighth-century England, mutual influence would by no means have been impossible)[31] but that no early medieval music, as far as we know, had isochronous measures. The very development of such measures, by Reese's interpretation, would have been implausible during the period of monophonic music preceding the thirteenth century. Historically, the development of measured music resulted from the need to keep voices together as part-music became increasingly complex:

From early organum straight through to the growth of a mensural system we really have part of but one development. And this development was primarily rhythmical—even when it dealt with unmeasured organum (itself merely a stage in the evolution towards a measured discant)—for it dealt with a new way of weaving designs in time, designs different in nature from those contemporaneously applied to plainsong. ... The creation of a mensural system, therefore, constituted a revolutionary step in music history, a step more difficult of achievement and hardly less important than the creation of the staff.[32]

Even if one disregards the historical objections to Pope's theory, one must have doubts about a system that consistently requires a non-linguistic unit to complete two of the five types of verse— about one-third of the 6,364 verses in *Beowulf*. Such a system of poetry or song is unlike any other system, so far as I am aware, in any language, ancient, medieval, or modern. Pope is right in demanding that a theory of verse-form reveal the order and equivalence that separate poetry from "loosely patterned prose."[33] But in suggesting that the equivalence must either be "syllabic equivalence" or "rhythmic equivalence," he fails to exhaust the possibilities; it does not follow that Old English verses, which obviously have unequal numbers of syllables, must therefore have equal measures. The import of the next six chapters is that metrical order does exist in Old English poetry, and it results from counting neither syllables nor measures. The units that are counted *contain* syllables, always one or more. Before explaining that unit, in Chapter Seven, it is necessary to proceed inductively and deal with a number of initially independent but ultimately related problems. The first of these problems, the minimum number of stresses in each verse, is the subject of Chapter Two.

NOTES

[1] W. K. Wimsatt, Jr., and Monroe C. Beardsley, "The Concept of Meter: An Exercise in Abstraction," *PMLA*, 74 (1959), 585–98.

[2] A long syllable is one containing a vowel long in quantity (*þā*) or a short vowel if the syllable is closed by a consonant (*wæd*); short syllables usually occur only in polysyllabic words (*wĭga*).

[3] The verse cited is *Beowulf* 68a. All line references in my text are to *Beowulf* unless otherwise noted; the edition is *Beowulf and the Fight at Finnsburg*, ed. Fr. Klaeber, 3rd ed. (Boston: Heath, 1950). I have omitted punctuation at the ends of the lines.

4 See Eduard Sievers, *Altgermanische Metrik* (Halle: Niemeyer, 1893), pp. 18–49. Throughout, I have grouped Sievers' D1, D2, and D3 under the label D1—the traditional grouping. What I call D2 (and attribute to Sievers as D2) is actually his D4.

5 Wimsatt and Beardsley, p. 592. See also Paull F. Baum, "The Character of Anglo-Saxon Verse," *MP*, 28 (1930), 155: ". . . the simple fact remains that the only metrical pattern in Anglo-Saxon verse is the two stresses to the line, with light syllables variously placed." See also C. L. Wrenn, "On the Continuity of English Poetry," *Anglia*, 76 (1958), 41–59; Joseph Malof, "The Native Rhythm of English Meters," *Texas Studies in Literature and Language*, 5 (1964), 582–85; and John Nist, "Metrical Uses of the Harp in *Beowulf*," in *Old English Poetry: Fifteen Essays*, ed. Robert P. Creed (Providence, R.I.: Brown University Press, 1967), pp. 27–31.

6 A similar pattern, which I would recognize as an exception to my statement, occurs once in *Beowulf*: in verse 1563a, the final syllable bears secondary linguistic stress:

$$x \quad x \, ' \qquad x \quad ' \, \smile x \, \backslash$$
Hē gefēng þā fetelhilt

John C. Pope—*The Rhythm of Beowulf*, 2nd ed. rev. (New Haven: Yale University Press, 1966), p. 261—suggests the possible deletion of *hē*. See also pp. 35–37, below.

7 As I shall argue in Chapter Three, pp. 37–43, below.

8 J. P. Oakden, *Alliterative Poetry in Middle English* (1930–35; rpt. [Hamden, Conn.] Archon, 1968), I, 174–76.

9 Northrop Frye, *Anatomy of Criticism: Four Essays* (1957; rpt. New York: Atheneum, 1966), pp. 251–52.

10 Wimsatt and Beardsley say that the lines in isolation *could* be read as strong-stress meter (p. 592).

11 A. J. Bliss, *The Metre of Beowulf*, 2nd ed. rev. (Oxford: Blackwell, 1967), pp. 61–68.

12 Marjorie Daunt, "Old English Verse and English Speech Rhythm," *Transactions of the Philological Society* (1946), p. 56.

13 Ibid., p. 64. See also A. J. Bliss, "The Appreciation of Old English Metre," in *English and Medieval Studies Presented to J. R. R. Tolkien*, ed. Norman Davis and C. L. Wrenn (London: Allen and Unwin, 1962), p. 29: "Whereas in most types of verse the metrical patterns are arbitrary, in Old English verse they are not: the metrical patterns are selected from among the rhythms which occur most commonly in natural speech."

14 Samuel Jay Keyser, "Old English Prosody," *College English*, 30 (1969), 331–56. It is important to read Keyser's essay in conjunction with an earlier "companion piece" that he wrote with Morris Halle, "Chaucer and the Study of Prosody," *College English*, 28 (1966), 187–219.

15 James Sledd, "Old English Prosody: A Demurrer," *College English*, 31 (1969), 73–74.

16 Chapter Four is wholly devoted to the important question of intermediate stress, and a key part of Chapter Seven concerns the necessity of four metrical positions (to be filled by at least four syllables) to the half-line. The matter of syllabic length is treated more briefly, in a discussion of resolution in Chapter Six, pp. 80–81, below.

17 Pope, *Rhythm*, pp. xiv–xv.

18 Keyser, "Old English Prosody," p. 352.

[19] Ibid., p. 332.

[20] See Pope, *Rhythm*, pp. 238–46. For further discussion of why certain pauses are a part of meter and not of performance, see Thomas Cable, "Timers, Stressers, and Linguists: Contention and Compromise," *MLQ*, 33 (1972), 227–39.

[21] John C. Pope, *Selections from Beowulf* (Pleasantville, N.Y.: Educational Audio Visual, Inc.).

[22] See, for example, Ritchie Girvan, rev. of Pope, *Rhythm*, *RES*, 19 (1943), 74.

[23] Pope, *Rhythm*, pp. 20–21.

[24] John C. Pope, ed., *Seven Old English Poems* (New York: Bobbs-Merrill, 1966), p. 117.

[25] Robert P. Creed, "A New Approach to the Rhythm of *Beowulf*," *PMLA*, 81 (1966), 23–33.

[26] Pope, *Rhythm*, p. x.

[27] R. B. Le Page, "A Rhythmical Framework for the Five Types," *English and Germanic Studies*, 6 (1957), 92–94.

[28] Gustave Reese, *Music in the Middle Ages* (New York: Norton, 1940), p. 276.

[29] See Paull F. Baum, "The Meter of the *Beowulf*," *MP*, 46 (1948), 74–75; Bliss, *Metre*, p. 107; and Josef Taglicht, "*Beowulf* and Old English Verse Rhythm," *RES*, n.s. 12 (1961), 342–44.

[30] Pope, *Rhythm*, p. x.

[31] See Peter Clemoes, *Liturgical Influence on Punctuation in Late Old English and Early Middle English Manuscripts*, Occasional Papers, No. 1 (Cambridge: Department of Anglo-Saxon, 1952); and Jess B. Bessinger, Jr., "The Sutton Hoo Harp Replica and Old English Musical Verse," in *Old English Poetry: Fifteen Essays*, ed. Robert P. Creed (Providence, R.I.: Brown University Press, 1967), pp. 5–6.

[32] Reese, *Music*, pp. 292–93.

[33] Pope, *Rhythm*, pp. xi–xii.

TWO

The Number of Stresses in an Old English Verse

We have seen that traditional two-stress theories of Old English meter as they are commonly interpreted leave much unexplained. An adequate statement of the meter cannot permit unstressed syllables to fall freely around two main stresses, for if that were possible, one would expect to find many syntactic patterns that do not occur or occur only rarely. The two-stress idea has its virtues, to be sure, one of which is the rejection of verses with only a single stress. The present chapter argues that this feature ought to be retained in any alternative system: the meter must specify *at least* two metrical stresses to the half-line. This rather negative statement, which falls far short of characterizing the Old English verse and which taken by itself misleads, must be made and supported in order to clear the ground of the "light verses" that Bliss describes and which several other scholars have accepted.

By Bliss's count, there are 1,358 one-stress, or light, verses in *Beowulf*.[1] Before his theory appeared, a small number of these verses were troublesome in requiring the metrist to wrest (in Bliss's words) a second main stress from among the particles. I shall argue that the embarrassment of having to give an occasional metrical stress to a syllable that in ordinary discourse would not require it is small compared with the embarrassment of assuming that a one-stress pattern is a perfectly normal and acceptable pattern.

According to Bliss, approximately one in every five verses of

Beowulf contains only one full stress. The light types fall into six categories, *a*, *d*, and *e*, which correspond to the three normal types, A, D, and E, and *A*, *D*, and *E* (capital letters, italicized), which also correspond to the normal types except for one characteristic: each verse of the latter three types consists of a single compound word. The present chapter will deal mainly with types *a* and *d*, and try to show that statements about type *d* account also for the three compound types.[2]

Critics of Bliss's theory have questioned his reading of specific structures but have generally accepted, or have been hesitant to reject altogether, the concept of the light verse. Winfred P. Lehmann, in his review of *The Metre of Beowulf*, pointed out that eighth-century Old English may have retained the Indo-European tendency to stress the verb when initial in its clause.[3] This tendency would cast doubt upon Bliss's scansion of a line such as 1013a:

ald   x   x   x   x   ′   x
1013a   Bugon þā tō bence   blædāgande

Following Lehmann's suggestion, Elinor D. Clemons in her dissertation and in an article with Rudolph Willard rescanned a number of verses beginning with verbs.[4] I view these criticisms as sound arguments against Bliss's theory and suggest that they are deficient only in not pushing the matter far enough. Lehmann's historical observation gives the Willard-Clemons study a basis for making the stressed initial verb a possible reading, though not a necessary one. Clemons credits Bliss with "logical and metrical explanations for the light, one-stress lines,"[5] and she and Willard accept Bliss's scansion of verse 257a (p. 231):

d1b   x   x   ′ x   x
257a   tō gecȳðanne,   hwanan ēowre cyme syndon

A recent use of Bliss's light verse is in a generative model of Old English prosody by S. J. Keyser, who describes three-stress *lines* as fully metrical, though technically complex.[6] Keyser presents a convincing argument for scanning verse 262a, *Wæs mīn fæder*, with one stress, but this verse has long been recognized as anomalous (see Bliss, p. 61), and seems insufficient for establishing a principle that would apply to more than a thousand verses in *Beowulf*. The other two verses that Keyser presents arguments for are type *dl* with secondary stress (3a, 38a), which I shall consider later in this chapter.

At least two studies have approached the problem of light verses from syntax. Willard and Clemons have rescanned nearly 200 verses introduced by verbs, and I have made a more limited study of introductory particles.[7] In each case, the great majority of verses were those that Bliss had scanned as light *a*. Although my concern was to show that *þā* in certain structures was an adverb rather than a subordinating conjunction, I found independent evidence for assigning it metrical stress. On that evidence, I revised Bliss's scansion to accord with Sievers' original reading:

Revised	´	x x	´	x	
Bliss a1c	x	x x	´	x	
53a	Đā wæs on burgum			Bēowulf Scyldinga	

The same method may be applied to all verses of type *a*, regardless of their syntactic structure. Bliss divides the 356 type *a* verses into ten subgroups containing the following patterns—given here with a representative line, Bliss's scansion, and a proposed revision. Many of these also occur in the Willard–Clemons study; in all instances my scansion accords with theirs. I shall give the revisions first, and then the reasons for so revising:

Revised	´ x ´ x		
Bliss a1b	x x ´ x		
2977a	Lēt se hearda	Higelāces þegn	

Revised	´ x x ´ x	
Bliss a1c	x x x ´ x	
1807a	Heht þā se hearda	Hrunting beran

Revised	´‿x x x ´ x	
Bliss a1d	x x x x ´ x	
1013a	Bugon þā tō bence	blǣdāgande

Revised	´ xx x x ´ x	
Bliss a1e	x xx x x ´ x	
590a	Secge ic þē tō sōðe,	sunu Ecglāfes

Revised   x x ′ x x   x ′ x
Bliss a1f   x x x   x x   x ′ x
1711a   ne geweōx hē him tō willan,   ac tō wælfealle

Revised   ′ x x   ′   ＼
Bliss a2c   x x x   ′   ＼
1506a   Bær þā sēo brimwyl[f],   þā hēo tō botme cōm

Revised   ′ x x x ′   ＼
Bliss a2d   x x x x ′   ＼
2593a   Hyrte hyne hordweard,   hreðer æðme wēoll

Revised   ′   x x   x x   ′ ＼
Bliss a2e   x   x x   x x   ′ ＼
2661a   Wōd þā þurh þone wælrēc,   wīgheafolan bær

Revised   ′ x x x x x x ′ ◡x ＼
Bliss a2f   x x x x x x x ′ ◡x ＼
2466a   nō ðȳ ær hē þone heaðorinc   hatian ne meahte

Revised   ′ x x x x x x x ′   ＼
Bliss a2g   x x x x x x x x ′   ＼
2172a   Hȳrde ic þæt hē ðone healsbēah   Hygde gesealde

Except for verses 2977a and 2466a, each of the above verses has double alliteration. Bliss argues that alliteration on the first syllable is accidental, an argument that deserves consideration: given a limited number of initial sounds, one can indeed expect accidental alliteration.

Bliss's own tables (pp. 122–24), however, contain much revealing information. All 356 verses of type *a* occur in the first half-line, and none occurs in the second. The reason is clear: light verses must have alliteration on the stress that Bliss marks, or there would be no alliteration at all to bind the two half-lines together. Although verses identical in structure to "light verses" occur in the second half-line, Bliss does not call them light. If he did, the pattern of alliteration would flatly contradict his analysis: alliteration in the second half-line must occur in the *first* metrically stressed syllable, the one that Bliss always ignores. Without this check in the first half-line (where either or both of the stresses may alliterate), one can present an analysis denying hundreds of stresses that actually occur. Thus, in the following b-verse, Bliss is obliged to recognize stress on the finite verb (or else the verse would have no alliteration):

Bliss 1A*1b   ′ x| x x ′ x
90b   swutol sang scopes.   Sægde sē þe cūþe

But in the a-verse, even with double alliteration, Bliss feels no need to stress the verb:

Bliss a1e   x x x x x ′ x
590a   Secge ic þē tō sōðe,   sunu Ecglāfes

To reconstruct the process by which one might arrive at the concept of light verse is not difficult. Bliss noticed, as others have, that the modern reader often has difficulty assigning stress in those verses where the first stressed syllable fails to alliterate. Such verses with single alliteration Bliss calls "light" and scans with a single stress. With a dozen light patterns, one can scan a large number of verses—especially if the concept is then extended to apply even to verses with double alliteration, such as those with initial verbs.

All of this is not to deny that there are verses in which the stress is less than obvious. But if a principle is established in the great majority of lines, it is reasonable to assume that ambiguous verses are constructed upon that same principle instead of upon a completely new one. If the principle requires a minimum of two stresses to the verse, it is reasonable again to assume that the poet and his audience felt two stresses in those occasional verses where the stress is less obvious to the modern reader.

If the critique sketched here is sufficient to reject the light *a* verse (the most common of the light types), one is left with Bliss's types *d, e,* and those light verses that consist of a single word, *A, D,* and *E* (the labels italicized). Of *e,* which applies to only seven verses, Bliss himself says: "It must be considered doubtful whether this type has any genuine existence" (p. 61). Much more common is type *d;* an explanation of this pattern will also tell us something about types *A, D,* and *E,* for the problem in all four patterns has to do with secondary stress. What Bliss considers a light variety of Sievers' D might better be called a light C. The typical pattern occurs in the first line of *Beowulf*:

Bliss d3a   x ′ ˘ x
1b   HWÆT, WĒ GĀR-DEna   in gēardagum

Of the five subtypes of the *d* variety, four have secondary stress by Bliss's classification: subtypes *d2*, *d3*, *d4*, and *d5*, which are credited with describing 464 of the total 691 type *d* verses. More interesting, however, is the one subtype that Bliss reads *without* secondary stress: *d1*, represented by 227 verses. Of these, 66 are inflected proper names containing three or more syllables—types which the grammars and handbooks specifically describe as having secondary stress: Alistair Campbell gives *Hrōþgar*, but *Hrōþgāres*.[8] In accordance with the traditional view, one might revise all 66 instances by inserting a secondary stress, as in the following:

Revised   x   ′ ˋ x
Bliss d1a   x   ′ x x
461a   mid Wilfingum;   ðā hine *Wede*ra cyn

Revised   x   x   ′ ˋ x
Bliss d1b   x   x   ′ x x
335b   heresceafta hēap?   Ic eom Hrōðgāres

Revised   x   x   x   ′ ˋ x
Bliss d1c   x   x   x   ′ x x
1272a   ond him tō Anwaldan   āre gelȳfde

Revised   x x x x ′ ˋ x
Bliss d1d   x x x x ′ x x
609b   brego Beorht-Dena;   gehȳrde on Bēowulfe

Another large group of *d1* verses consists of compounds. The grammars assign secondary stress to compounds in which the two parts retain their original semantic force. Of linguistic facts that can be reconstructed only with uncertainty, "semantic force" is surely among the most difficult. Although the manuscripts offer no help, A. J. Wyatt, in the edition later revised by R. W. Chambers, inserted hyphens in compounds when he felt that both parts retained their full meanings.[9] His reading suggests that seventeen of the verses in question contain secondary stress, verses such as the following:

Revised		x x ′‿x ＼ x
Bliss d1b		x x ′‿x x x
969b	feorh-ʒeniðlan;	wæs tō fore-mihtiʒ

Revised	x x ′ ＼ x	
Bliss d1b	x x ′ x x	
2197a	on ðām lēod-scipe	lond ʒecynde

Revised	x x x ′ ＼ x	
Bliss d1c	x x x ′ x x	
2373a	Nō ðȳ ǣr fēa-sceafte	findan meahton

Revised		x x ′ ＼ x
Bliss d1b		x x ′ x x
2999b	Þæt ys sīo fǣhðo	ond se fēond-scipe

Semantic considerations aside, all seventeen verses receive stress by another rule of the grammar, whereby the second element of *any* compound receives secondary stress if it is disyllabic or inflected (see Campbell, p. 34).

Similarly, the grammars assign secondary stress to derivative suffixes such as -*ing* in inflected forms. Eight verses contain inflected *æþeling*, two have *gædeling*:

Revised	x x ′‿x ＼ x	
Bliss d1b	x x ′‿x x x	
982a	siþðan æþelingas	eorles cræfte

Revised	x ′‿x ＼ x	
Bliss d1a	x ′‿x x x	
2617a	his gædelinges	gūðgewǣdu

The superlative suffix -*est* also qualifies for stress when medial; twelve of the *d1* verses are of this type, six of them containing *sēlestan*. The same words tend to occur in similar metrical environments:

Revised	x ′ ＼ x	
Bliss d1a	x ′ x x	
416a	þā sēlestan,	snotere ceorlas

Eleven more *dl* verses contain the suffix *-enne* of the inflected infinitive:

Revised	x x ′ ˋ x	
Bliss d1b	x x ′ x x	
1851a	tō gecēosenne	cyning ǣnigne

At this point, it should be possible to draw the following conclusion: by one rule or another, all 227 verses scanned by Bliss as *dl* can be revised to contain a secondary stress; in most cases, more than one rule applies. Since some of these rules are based on metrical criteria as well as on strictly phonological criteria, one runs the risk of apparent circularity: of justifying Sievers' metrical system through appeal to grammatical rules that are based, in part, upon that system.

A completely independent argument is possible, however. In order to develop that argument, I shall begin outlining an alternative to Bliss's system—one in which the terms are redefined and the restrictions differently stated. I shall assume that metrical ictus constitutes something different from what it is usually taken to be. To the extent that deductions drawn from that assumption avoid the difficulties already noted without incurring others, the alternative argues against the idea of the light verse. Specifically, I propose that the following is a necessary but not a sufficient condition for a long syllable (or its resolved equivalent) to have metrical ictus:

CONDITION: A syllable can bear metrical ictus only if it has greater linguistic prominence than at least one adjacent syllable.

To avoid misunderstanding, we should dwell upon two points. The first is the distinction between linguistic prominence and metrical ictus.[10] Trager-Smith phonology found four significant degrees of linguistic stress in Modern English, while current generative phonology computes many more. When statements are made about an iambic pentameter line as *verse*, however, instead of as *language*, the various degrees of linguistic stress are usually reduced to two—and rightly so, I believe.[11]

A second and related point is that only adjacent syllables are compared, and the important fact is whether a given syllable is more prominent than one which precedes or follows it. The observation has often been made that we judge without much accuracy the relative prominence of widely separated syllables, and it has been hypothesized that only the comparison of adjacent syllables is metrically relevant in any event.[12] One consequence of assuming that hypothesis, as I do here, is that a syllable described as containing secondary stress may have no metrical ictus at all:

                                   ′ ⌣x x x x   ′   x
1441b   gryrelīcne gist.   Gyrede hine Bēowulf

Although one may consider -*wulf* to have the linguistic value of secondary stress, as Pope does, it fails to meet the condition for metrical stress because it comes at the end of the verse after a more prominent syllable. In order for -*wulf* to qualify for metrical stress in the terms that I have proposed, it should be followed by a

                                         ′ ∧ x
weakly stressed inflectional syllable: *Bēowulfes*. The syllable -*wulf*- is now more prominent than the syllable that follows. Such syllables I shall refer to as having intermediate stress, leaving the concept of secondary stress (with which I wish to avoid confusion) for linguistic description.

The evidence for accepting the view of metrical ictus that I have proposed is also evidence against the light verse, for the proposed view readily explains certain curious facts that otherwise would have no immediate explanation. In particular, the following pattern occurs in the verse of Middle and Modern English, but not in *Beowulf*: x (x) ⌣́ ⌣́, with two final stresses. Thus, in *Sir Gawain and the Green Knight*, one finds:

                                                     ′   ′
And neuenes hit his aune nome, as hit now hat[13]

And in *Macbeth*:

              ′   x ‵ x ′   ′
        Toad, that under cold stone[14]

But in *Beowulf* there are no verses of the form:

$$\overset{\text{x} \quad \text{x} \quad \prime \quad \prime}{\text{*þær wæs wældrēor}}$$

$$\overset{\text{x} \quad \text{x} \quad \prime \quad \prime}{\text{*þæt wæs fȳrheard}}[15]$$

Syntactically, there is no reason for the pattern not to occur. One finds:

11b	gomban gyldan; $\overset{\text{x} \quad \text{x} \quad \prime \quad \prime \quad \text{x}}{\text{þæt wæs gōd cyning}}$
856b	beornas on blancum. $\overset{\text{x} \quad \text{x} \quad \prime \quad \prime \quad \text{x}}{\text{Đǣr wæs Bēowulfes}}$

but not:

$$\overset{\text{x} \quad \text{x} \quad \prime \quad \prime}{\text{*þæt wæs gōd þegn}}$$

$$\overset{\text{x} \quad \text{x} \quad \prime \quad \prime}{\text{*Đǣr wæs Bēowulf}}$$

One can plausibly explain these facts by assuming the condition for metrical stress that I have proposed above, and two such metrical stresses to the verse. By Sievers' system *þegn* would qualify as a metrical stress and a monosyllabic foot in certain contexts, but not after a foot such as x x ⏌. The fact that x x ⏌ plus ⏌ cannot occur in Sievers' system is an accidental fact, but within the system proposed here, the fact follows naturally: the second stress is not a stress at all unless it is more prominent than the first stress. While it is obvious that *drēor* in the compound *wældrēor* is less strongly stressed than the preceding syllable, verses that end in heavily stressed syllables other than compounds (such as an adjective plus a noun) are more difficult. In Chapter Five, I shall argue that the first of two clashing stresses in Old English verse must *always* be heavier, compound or not—a constraint that applies to the verse of Old English, but not to that of Middle and Modern English. If my argument is valid, then taken together with the condition that I have set upon metrical stress, we have an explanation for why the above patterns appear in Middle and Modern English, but not earlier, and a third argument against the light verse.

This chapter has argued that each verse of Old English poetry contains at least two metrical stresses. Although Bliss finds two types of light verse containing a single stress (*a* and *e*) and four types containing a main stress plus a secondary stress (*d* and italicized *A*, *D*, and *E*), the fact that all 363 of the first two varieties occur in the first half-line suggests that an initial metrical stress in each instance has been ignored. If the two types without secondary stress are rescanned as normal, and if the one subtype of *d* that Bliss reads without secondary stress can be shown to have it, then the claim that the 995 verses in types *d*, *A*, *D*, and *E* are light is an empty claim: to say that a verse must have two metrical stresses unless it has one metrical stress plus a secondary stress is simply another way of saying that all verses must have two metrical stresses, and in some contexts a secondary linguistic stress may count as one of the metrical stresses. Finally, one may propose a necessary condition for the occurrence of metrical stress. The fact that there are no patterns of the form x (x) $\perp$ $\perp$ is consistent with the proposed condition and also with arguments against the light verse.

NOTES

[1] A. J. Bliss, *The Metre of Beowulf*, 2nd ed. rev. (Oxford: Blackwell, 1967), p. 122.

[2] A problem of terminology is the possible confusion of a-verse (the first half-line) with type *a* (the light variety of Sievers' type A). I shall refer to the first half-line with a hyphen and the word *verse* and the light variety with no hyphen and the word *type*. Although Bliss does not italicize types *a*, *d*, and *e*, I shall do so when reference is made to them within the text.

[3] Winfred P. Lehmann, rev. of Bliss, *Metre, JEGP*, 59 (1960), 139–40.

[4] See Elinor D. Clemons, "A Metrical Analysis of the Old English Poem *Exodus*," Ph. D. dissertation, University of Texas, 1961; see also Rudolph Willard and Elinor D. Clemons, "Bliss's Light Verses in the *Beowulf*," *JEGP*, 66 (1967), 230–44.

[5] Clemons, "Metrical," p. 12.

[6] Samuel Jay Keyser, "Old English Prosody," *College English*, 30 (1969), 331–56.

[7] Thomas Cable, "Rules for Syntax and Metrics in *Beowulf*," *JEGP*, 69 (1970), 81–88.

[8] A. Campbell, *Old English Grammar*, rev. ed. (Oxford: Clarendon Press, 1962), p. 34.

[9] A. J. Wyatt and R. W. Chambers, eds., *Beowulf with the Finnsburg Fragment* (1914; rpt. Cambridge: Cambridge University Press, 1952).

10 I use the terms *metrical ictus* and *metrical stress* interchangeably. An important distinction between *linguistic prominence* and *linguistic stress* is drawn in Chapter Eight, p. 97, below.

11 W. K. Wimsatt, Jr., and Monroe C. Beardsley make this point well in "The Concept of Meter: An Exercise in Abstraction," *PMLA*, 74 (1959), 593.

12 See, for example, Otto Jespersen, "Notes on Metre," in his *Linguistica: Selected Papers in English, French and German* (Copenhagen: Levin and Munksgaard, 1933), pp. 255–56.

13 Line 10, from the edition by J. R. R. Tolkien and E. V. Gordon, 2nd ed. rev. Norman Davis (Oxford: Clarendon Press, 1968).

14 IV.i.6. Cited by George R. Stewart, Jr., in *The Technique of English Verse* (New York: Holt, 1930), p. 63. See also John Masefield's, "The West Wind": "It's a
x x   ′   ′
warm wind, the west wind, full of birds' cries."

15 Bliss finds five verses of the type x x x ⌣́ ⌣́, and 21 others with four to seven unstressed syllables at the beginning, but in each case he ignores the first stress:

Revised		′	x	x		x x		′	﹨
Bliss a2e		x	x	x		x x		′	﹨
2661a		Wōd þā þurh þone wælrēc,						wīgheafolan bær	

THREE

Constraints on Anacrusis in Type A

The most common of all metrical patterns in *Beowulf* is Sievers' A: ⏌ x ⏌ x. Type A with one or more unstressed syllables at the beginning is a rather rare variant of the basic type, traditionally described as "type A with anacrusis"—schematically, x ⏌ x ⏌ x, or, in W. W. Greg's notation, ∿ ⏌ ∿ ⏌ ∿.[1] An array of statistical facts that I shall present below supports Sievers' view that anacrusis was a severely restricted metrical feature. The same facts point toward a syntactic constraint that has not been generally noticed before, and which applies to as many as two-thirds of this metrical subtype in *Beowulf*. The conclusion that I draw leads to a reconsideration of the theory within which I have gathered the evidence, and to an objection. Specifically, Sievers' classification of metrical types relegates to an inconspicuous place a pervasive principle of Old English prosody. The fact that the poet generally avoided the five-position pattern ∿ ⏌ ∿ ⏌ ∿ should be stated first, I would claim, even before naming the Five Types, for the avoidance of that pattern is a basic part of the poet's craft.

This chapter consists, then, of two parts. First I shall argue that the facts which Sievers has presented with respect to anacrusis are correct. If the unstressed syllables at the beginning of type A with anacrusis are metrically equivalent to other stretches of unstressed syllables (if *ge-* at the beginning of verse 505a, for example, is the same kind of metrical entity as *-um* at the end), then this type of verse would have five positions, or members, or, in Sievers' terminology, five *Glieder:*

~ ⁄   ~   ⁄   ~
A   x ⁄ x x   x   ⁄‿x x
505a   gehēde under heofenum   þonne hē sylfa

In fact, I would argue, as Sievers does,[2] that the initial syllable is not at all the same as the other unstressed syllables, that it is an addition to the basic pattern, analogous perhaps to the grace note in music, and that there are clear restrictions upon the kind of syllable that can form what appears to be a fifth position of a verse. In restating Sievers' view, I mean to take issue with later interpretations, such as Keyser's, that do not pay close attention to the constraint that Sievers stated, and I shall try to support my view with original data that indicate a general syntactic restriction.

All of this leads to a second conclusion—that Sievers' system, though it covers the facts very well, does not place the emphasis where it belongs and is therefore less than theoretically optimal. I shall compare the poetry with passages of prose to draw what I take to be the most interesting conclusion of this chapter: a description of a basic difference between Old English poetry and Old English prose.

The number of A verses with anacrusis in *Beowulf* has been calculated differently by different scholars. Sievers lists 13 of the type, Bliss 27, and Pope 121.[3] Since Pope's count includes all of the verses cited by Sievers and all but two of the verses cited by Bliss, his list may be taken as the fullest survey of possible five-position verses. To these, one may add two verses that Klaeber cites, to give a total of 125.

Although *Beowulf* contains over 6,000 verses, 125 possible occurrences of the pattern $\sim \perp \sim \perp \sim$ are too many to ignore. One might argue that the five-position type, while clearly a minor one, is well enough represented to justify its inclusion with the other five patterns. However, many of the verses share characteristics that are worth considering as clues to an alternative explanation. Thirty-one of them, for example, begin with the syllable *ge-*.[4] Verses 217a and 675a are representative:

~   ⁄   ~   ⁄   ~
217a   Gewāt þā ofer wǣgholm   winde gefӯsed

675a Gespræc þā se gōda   gylpworda sum

Nine verses begin with the negative particle *ne*, as in lines 1612 and 1659:[5]

1612a Ne nōm hē in þǣm wīcum,   Weder-Gēata lēod

1659a Ne meahte ic æt hilde   mid Hruntinge

Three verses have disyllabic anacrusis consisting of *ne* plus *ge-*:

109a ne gefeah hē þǣre fǣhðe,   ac hē hine feor forwræc

1011a Ne gefrægen ic þā mǣgþe   māran weorode

1711a ne gewēox hē him tō willan,   ac tō wælfealle

Eighteen verses begin with one of six verbal prefixes: *ā-* (6), *on-* (5), *for-* (3), *of-* (2), *be-* (1), and *æt-* (1).[6] Verses 399a, 1518a, and 1758a are typical:

399a Ārās þā se rīca,   ymb hine rinc manig

1518a Ongeat þā se gōda   grundwyrgenne

1758a Bebeorh þē ðone bealonīð,   Bēowulf lēofa

In addition to verses beginning with verbal prefixes, there are twenty-two possible five-position verses that have five positions only because one of the syllables named above occurs in the middle of the verse—for example, lines 666, 1223, and 1504:[7]

666b Grendle tōgēanes,   swā guman gefrungon

1223b efne swā sīde   swā sǣ bebūgeð

1504b þæt hēo þone fyrdhom   ðurhfōn ne mihte

All of this information can be summarized briefly: a limited number of verbal prefixes (and the negative particle) occur in eighty-three verses, or two-thirds of the type A verses that might possibly have five positions. Interestingly, all of these syllables except *ne* also occur in the rule for word stress in Old English. As in the other Germanic languages, it is the first syllable of the word in Old English that regularly receives stress. The major exception is the class of compound verbs beginning with what some grammarians call prepositional adverbs—syllables such as *ā-*, *on-*, *for-*.[8] In Germanic, these syntactic combinations were not single words at the time that stress was fixed; subsequently, they developed into compound words with stress on the second element.

Since certain syllables occur repeatedly in the poetry, it is possible that the simplest statement of the meter would be one that limited verses to four positions unless the fifth position was filled specifically by a verbal prefix. This statement is analogous to the simplest formulation of the Germanic stress rule, which assigns stress to the first syllable of words except to the very syllables under discussion here. The fact that the same prefixes must be listed in two different systems suggests that they form a natural class with regard to stress—an assumption not without plausibility, for if any group of syllables in Old English is to be considered exceptional in the assignment of stress, these syllables, phonetically slight as they are, are likely prospects. I refrain from drawing the obvious generalization because of certain problems that result. To say that the syntactic rule would cover two-thirds of the possible five-position verses leaves the other third unaccounted for. Also, it is a fact that the exceptional prefixes are essential in such verses as 2516a: *Gegrētte ðā*. For this curious fact, I have no explanation.[9]

Of the forty-two verses yet to be considered, seven should be excluded because of emendations: 25a, 107a, 395b, 414a, 1068a, 2093a, and 2385a.[10] Most of the remaining thirty-five verses have five positions by Pope's reading but not by Bliss's.[11] One verse that Klaeber reads with anacrusis (v. 368a) Pope reads differently by marking the quantity of the *a* in *wīggetawum* as short rather than long (p. 322). Verse 2481b has five positions only when scanned as in the first edition of Pope's study; in the 1966 edition, he divides

the line differently (to accord with Klaeber's division) and elimi-
nates the anacrusis (p. xxix).

A plausible case could be made for stressing the first syllable in
several of the verses, giving them four positions instead of five.
Willard and Clemons scan 506a with a stress on the verb:[12]

```
Willard          ′    x  x   ′   x
Pope       | (′)        ‿  |  ⁄⁄  ⁖ |
506a             Eart þū sē Bēowulf,    sē þe wið Brecan wunne
```

And I have argued that the adverb *þā* may receive metrical
stress:[13]

```
Revised       ′  x  x  x   x ′ x
Pope        | ′        ‿   |  ⁄⁄ ‿ |
47a           Þā gӯt hīe him āsetton      segen g(yl)denne
```

Pope notes that some verses which he reads with five positions may
have a different scansion (pp. 265–66)—specifically, that the first
syllable of 71a (which alliterates) and of 355a (with transverse
alliteration) may be stressed:

```
Revised      ′    x  x   ′   x
Pope       | (′)      ‿   |⁄⁄  ‿ |
71a             ond þ r on innan     eall ged lan
```

```
Revised       ′   x  x   ′ x
Pope       | (′)     ‿  |  ⁄⁄ ‿|
355a            ðē mē se gōda      āgifan þenceð
```

A general observation applies to all of these thirty-five verses. If
they are metrically of the form ⌣ ⏌ ⌣ ⏌ ⌣, it is paradoxical that
they are the very verses that Bliss finds most amenable to his theory
of the "light" verse, a verse with only one stress, schematically
⌣ ⏌ ⌣. In fact, these verses are lighter than most, for they characteristically begin with two or three monosyllabic particles or other
weakly stressed syllables, as in 22a:

```
Bliss         x   x x x   ′  x
22a           þæt hine on ylde    eft gewunigen
```

It is not at all obvious which of the first three words, if any, should
receive metrical stress; Bliss argues that none should. But one
could give heavier stress to the personal pronoun, as Pope does,

and have a verse that is deviant for the opposite reason—for having too many metrical units. If one stresses *þæt*, on the other hand, as I would follow Sievers in doing, the verse is altogether normal. A solution to these difficult verses must be left for further study. In the absence of such a solution, I shall assume that all thirty-five are exceptions to the view being presented here—that *none*, in other words, receives metrical stress on the first syllable. Further, since it is the five-position verse, rather than Bliss's light verse, that contradicts the main part of the present argument, I shall assume Pope's reading.

The 125 verses that could be read with anacrusis fall, then, into several large groups. Eighty-three of them, or 66 percent, have five positions because of a verb with an initial unstressed syllable (or the particle *ne*). Seven are dubious because of emendations. Some of the remaining thirty-five could be scanned as normal A types by stressing the first syllable; of these, a more convincing case could be made for some than for others, but I shall assume that none have the normal four positions. The thirty-five verses amount to about one-half of 1 percent of the 6,364 verses in *Beowulf*. Even the full 125 that might conceivably be scanned as $\sim \perp \sim \perp \sim$ (by counting the verbal prefixes as occupying regular positions) amount to less than 2 percent. An interesting question might be posed as follows: How many verses of this type could one *expect* to occur, if one knew something about Old English syntax and nothing about the meter?

A comparison of the poetry with Wulfstan's prose suggests that one could expect considerably more patterns of the five-position type were it not for the meter; apparently it is the meter that screens out the pattern and keeps it from being more common than it is, for it is quite common in Wulfstan. The similarity between poetry of the eighth century and prose works of the bishop who died in 1023 has often been noted, most fully by Angus McIntosh, who divided a passage from the edition of A. S. Napier into half-lines and placed stress marks.[14] I have added the symbol $\sim$ to mark the theses:

$$\overset{\sim}{} \quad \overset{\prime}{} \quad \overset{\sim}{} \quad \overset{\prime}{} \quad \overset{\sim}{}$$

Ac þa beoð adwealde

　　～　　　′　　～　　′　　～
and þurh deofol beswicene

～　′　　～　′　～
þe þæs ne gelyfað

～　　′　　～　　～　　′
ac wenað þæt se man

～　′　　～　　′　～
scyle deadlice swyltan

′　～　　′　x
efne swa nyten

～　′　　～　　′　～
and syþþan ne þoljan

～　′　　～　　′　～
ne yrmðe ne myrhðe

～　　′　　′　～
ne ænig lean habban

′　～　　′　～
þæs ðe he worhte

～　′　～　′　x
on lifes fæce

～　　′　　～　　′　～
þa hwile þe he mehte

～　　′　　～　　′　x
Ac soþ is þæt ic secge

～　′　　～　′　～
of eorþan gewurdan

′　～　′　～
ærest geworhte

′　～　　′　～
þa ðe we sylfe

′　～　　′　x
ealle of coman

～　′　　～　　′　x
and to eorþan we scylan

′　～　′　～
ealle geweorþan

~ ⟋ ~ ⟋ ~
and syþþan habban

~ ⟋ ~ ⟋ ~
swa ece wite

⟋ ~ ⟋ ~
aa butan ende

~ ⟋ ~ ⟋ ~
swa ece blisse

~ ⟋ ~ ⟋ ~
swa hwæþer we on life

⟋ ~ ⟋ ~
æror geearnodon

⟋ ~ ⟋ ~
God ure helpe

The most striking fact about this passage is the one McIntosh notes: the way in which the prose divides naturally into two-stress phrases. The second most striking fact is the way that many of these phrases may be scanned with the pattern $\sim \perp \sim \perp \sim$. If vowel length is relevant, and resolution thus possible, twelve out of twenty-six (or just under 50 percent) of the two-stress phrases have a pattern that was avoided in the poetry. Of these, only one has a position filled by *ne, ge-*, or the other six prefixes: *þe þæs ne gelyfað*. If vowel length is not relevant in the prose, as McIntosh suggests, three more phrases may be added to give just over 50 percent. Either way, the situation differs widely from the poetry where, in *Beowulf*, fewer than 2 percent of the verses could conceivably have the five-position pattern.

The pattern is typical of longer passages as well. In the *Sermo ad Anglos*, McIntosh found that 352 out of 598 two-stress verses (or 59 percent) had five positions (pp. 133–34). The high proportion in Wulfstan's prose is less a characteristic of Wulstan than the lack of it in *Beowulf* is a characteristic of the poetry. W. J. Sedgefield has scanned a passage from the *Anglo-Saxon Chronicle* of 959, to which I have added the theses.[15] Although Greg, from whom I have borrowed the tilde, uses that notation to represent syllables with both weak and secondary stress, I have retained Sedgefield's markings of secondary stress in order to represent accurately his scansion, and have assigned the tilde only to those syllables that he left unmarked:

~   ′   ~   ′   ~   ′   ~
On his dagum hit godode georne,

~   ′   ~   ′   ~
and God him geuðe

~   ′   ~   ′   ~
þæt he wunode on sibbe

~   ′   ~   ′   ~
þa hwile þe he leofode;

~   ′   ~   ′   ＼
and he dyde swa him þearf wæs,

′   ~   ′   ~
earnode þes georne.

~   ′   ＼   ′   ~
He arerde Godes lof wide

~   ′   ＼   ′   ~
and Godes lage lufode

~   ′   ~   ＼   ′   ~
and folces frið bette

′   ~   ′   ~
swiðost þara cyninga

~   ′   ~   ′   ~
þe ær him gewurde

~   ′   ~   ′   ~
be manna gemynde,

~   ′   ~   ′   ~
and God him ec fylste

~   ′   ~   ′   ~
þæt ciningas and eorlas

′   ~   ′   ＼
georne him to bugon

~   ′   ~   ′   ~
and wurdon underþeodde;

/   ~   /   ~

eal he gewilde

/   ~   \   /   ~

þet he sylf wolde.

~   /   ~   /   ~

He wearð wide geond þeodland

/   ~   /   ~

swiðe geweorðod

~   /   ~   /   ~

for þam þe he weorðode

/   \   /   ~

Godes naman georne

~   /   \   /   ~

and Godes lage smeade

/   ~   /   ~

oft and gelome

~   /   \   /   ~

and Godes lof rærde

/   ~   /   ~

wide and side

~   /   ~   /   ~

and wislice rædde

/   ~   /   ~

oftost a simle

~   /   ~   /   ~

for Gode and for worulde

/   ~   /   ~

eall his þeode.

/   ~   /   ~

Ane misdæde

~   /   ~   /   ~

he dyde þeah to swiðe

/   ~   /   ~

þæt he ælþeodige

/   \   /   ~

unsida lufode

˜　ʹ　˜　ʹ　˜
and hæðene þeawas

ʹ　˜　ʹ　˜
innan þyssan lande

˜　ʹ　˜　ʹ　˜
gebrohte to fæste.

˜　ʹ　˜　ʹ　˜
Ac God him geunne

ʹ　˜　ˋ　ʹ　˜
þæt his goda dæda

ʹ　˜　ʹ　˜
swyðran weorðan

ʹ　˜　ʹ　˜
þonne misdæda

˜　ʹ　˜　ʹ　˜
his sawle to gescyldnesse

˜　ʹ　˜　ʹ　˜
on langsuman syðe.

Nineteen of the forty-three verses (or 44 percent) clearly have the pattern $\sim\perp\sim\perp\sim$, including one with the syllable *ge-* (l. 37): *gebrohte to fæste*. If one follows Greg in subsuming secondary stress under the tilde, five more lines could be added (ll. 5, 7, 8, 23, and 25), as in the following:

˜　ʹ　˜　ʹ　˜
and Godes lage smeade

Twenty-three of the verses (or 53 percent) would then have five positions.

A full explanation of the frequency of the five-position pattern would require a detailed analysis of the syntactic structures, but a partial explanation can be suggested: syntactically, the five-position pattern of the prose is the expected one. In ordinary formal discourse, many two-stress phrases would begin with an unstressed particle, preposition, or conjunction, and end on an unstressed inflectional syllable; thus:

˜　ʹ　˜　ʹ　˜
swa ece blisse

Although this would be a normal pattern for the poetry as well, it is avoided, for the meter excludes it. Otherwise one would expect to find the pattern in the same proportions in the poetry as in the prose—in which case *Beowulf* would contain over 3,000 verses of the type, rather than the 125 that might or might not be so read. However the meter is stated, it must contain an explicit constraint against the occurrence of the five-position type. Sievers' system, unlike Pope's, Bliss's, or Keyser's, contains such a constraint, but Sievers states it as a brief note about a subtype of one of his five types, obscuring the crucially interesting implications that it raises. If type A with anacrusis could occur freely, there is good reason, syntactically, for it to be the most common pattern; in fact, it is among the rarest, and two-thirds of the possible occurrences appear to have a common syntactic explanation.

NOTES

[1] W. W. Greg, "The 'Five Types' in Anglo-Saxon Verse," *Modern Language Review*, 20 (1925), 12–17. I shall follow Greg in using the tilde as a variable to represent any number of x or syllables with less than metrical stress.

[2] Eduard Sievers, "Zur Rhythmik des germanischen Alliterationsverses I," *Beiträge zur Geschichte der deutschen Sprache und Literatur*, 10 (1885), 234.

[3] Ibid.; A. J. Bliss, *The Metre of Beowulf*, 2nd ed. rev. (Oxford: Blackwell, 1967), p. 127; John C. Pope, *The Rhythm of Beowulf*, 2nd ed. rev. (New Haven: Yale University Press, 1966), pp. 254–74, 329. Since I have put Pope's findings to a use somewhat different from that which he intended, I should explain my interpretation of his data. The normal gradation of stress in his system, from heaviest to weakest, is ⸜, ⸝, ⸌, ⸍ (pp. 43–44, 246). Of primary interest here is the heaviest stressed syllable in each measure—whether ⸜, ⸝, or even (in the absence of any other stressed syllable) ⸍. Any syllables that precede the first stressed syllable of type A, I take to be anacrusis, following Sievers (although Pope applies the term only to those introductory syllables that precede the entire first measure).

[4] Verses 217a, 234a, 301a, 388a, 459a, 505a, 675a, 728a, 758a, 827a, 1125a, 1304a, 1425a, 1474a, 1537a, 1557a, 1732a, 1963a, 1977a, 2252a, 2417a, 2460a, 2529a, 2542a, 2606a, 2629a, 2659a, 2681a, 2703a, 2717a, and 2949a.

[5] Verses 1322a, 1612a, 1659a, 2609a, 2653a, 2697a, 2855a, 2971a, and 3079a.

[6] Verses 399a, 1108a, 1397a, 2538a, 3121a, 3141a, 409a, 1169a, 1518a, 2640a, 3143a, 1151a, 1751a, 1767a, 1545a, 1665a, 1758a, and 2878a.

[7] Verses 93b, 666b, 706b, 751a, 967a, 1082a, 1223b, 1347a, 1504b, 1661a, 1773b, 1846a, 1877b, 2195a, 2204a, 2247b, 2304a, 2592b, 2665a, 3009a, 3081a, and 3104a.

[8] See A. Campbell, *Old English Grammar*, rev. ed. (Oxford: Clarendon Press, 1962), p. 30.

[9] Max Kaluza formulates a rule entitled "Law Stating When Prefixes May Have a Beat," in *Englische Metrik in historischer Entwicklung dargestellt* (Berlin: Felber, 1909), pp. 56–57; trans. A. C. Dunstan, *A Short History of English Versification* (London: Allen, 1911), pp. 60–61. In effect, Kaluza counts prefixes when it is convenient within his system to do so, but no external evidence is presented in support of the law. See also Pope, *Rhythm*, pp. 57–58.

[10] On 25a, 107a, 414a, 1068a, and 2093a, see Bliss, *Metre*, pp. 41–42. On 395b and 2385a, see the notes in Klaeber's text.

[11] Verses 22a, 47a, 71a, 355a, 368a, 393a, 503a, 506a, 679a, 813a, 1059a, 1186a, 1248a, 1380a, 1477a, 1521a, 1549a, 1563a, 1566a, 1599a, 1777a, 1780a, 1834a, 1878a, 1972a, 1987a, 2104a, 2258a, 2481b, 2494a, 2651a, 2714a, 2716a, 2966a, and 3107a.

[12] Rudolph Willard and Elinor D. Clemons, "Bliss's Light Verses in the *Beowulf*," *JEGP*, 66 (1967), 236.

[13] Thomas Cable, "Rules for Syntax and Metrics in *Beowulf*," *JEGP*, 69 (1970), 81–88.

[14] Angus McIntosh, "Wulfstan's Prose," *Proceedings of the British Academy*, 35 (1949), 114–15.

[15] W. J. Sedgefield, *An Anglo-Saxon Book of Verse and Prose* (Manchester: Manchester University Press, 1928), p. 373.

FOUR

Intermediate Stress in Type E

Although there might be a consensus among those who work with Old English meter that many type E verses have secondary linguistic stress, there would be little agreement about how that level of stress should be treated in the meter: whether it should be recognized as a metrical fact at all, and if so, whether it should count as a full stress, or as a weak stress, or as something in between. A common solution is to divide the foot into two parts, an arsis and a thesis, and to mark the secondary stress as different from the weak stresses (⌣̱ instead of x) but to group it with them as a part of the thesis. Among those who adopt this solution, however, there is disagreement over which of the two features the theory should emphasize—the fact that the syllable with secondary stress is stronger than another syllable, or the fact that it is weaker.

Sievers makes it a third kind of unit in its own right,[1] and so does Jakob Schipper, who follows Sievers in always marking secondary stress and requiring it in certain contexts. But Schipper emphasizes its affinity with the light syllables rather than the heavy:

In these cases [such as *healærna mæst*] Sievers gives the verse-member with this secondary accent the character of a subordinate arsis, or beat (*Nebenhebung*). But it is better, in view of the strongly marked two-beat swing of the hemistich, to look on such members with a secondary accent as having only the rhythmical value of unaccented syllables, and to call them *theses* with a slight accent. The two-beat rhythm of the hemistich is its main characteristic, for though the two beats are not always of exactly equal force they are always prominently distinguished from the unaccented members of the hemistich, the rhythm of which would be marred by the introduction of an additional beat however slightly marked.[2]

Bliss uses secondary stress in compound nouns as a detail of classification, but he spends a full chapter refuting "Sievers' erroneous belief that there was metrical evidence of secondary stress on formative and derivative syllables,"[3] a view that leads Bliss to posit large categories of D and E verses without secondary stress beside those with it:

1D1	$\acute{-} \mid \acute{-} \times \times$
1D2	$\acute{-} \mid \acute{-} \grave{-} \times$
3E1	$\acute{-} \times \times \mid \acute{-}$
3E2	$\acute{-} \grave{-} \times \mid \acute{-}$

Secondary stress does not crucially characterize D and E verses in Bliss's system. Subtypes with and without it can be classified differently, but the two varieties belong to the same metrical type.

An extreme view of secondary stress as irrelevant to meter is that of S. J. Keyser, whose theory requires only that a *line* of Old English verse contain three or four stressed syllables and at least one unstressed syllable (after the first stress of the second half-line). By Keyser's rules, secondary stress need not occur at all, and if it does occur, phonetically, it does not count as such in the metrical scheme.[4]

Here, then, are four different views of secondary stress: Sievers and Schipper see it as essential in types D and E, but they differ over its relation to arsis and thesis. Bliss allows types D and E with only two levels of stress, but he finds contexts in which the intermediate level must occur. Keyser rejects the concept altogether and scans syllables with secondary stress as either fully stressed or weakly stressed, depending upon the other syllables in the line.

The purpose of the present chapter is to determine whether or not an intermediate level of metrical stress is essential in any verses of *Beowulf* and particularly in verses of type E. In stating the problem as I have, I am asking a somewhat different question from the questions posed by the other four theorists. In part, I

believe that the problem of secondary stress has not been satis-
factorily resolved because of confusion between the linguistic
concept and the metrical. By inquiring about intermediate
metrical stress, I am assuming the view of Chapter Two: for a
syllable to have metrical stress, it must have greater linguistic
prominence than at least one adjacent syllable. If at the same time
it has *less* prominence that its other adjacent syllable, it does not
cease to bear metrical stress, because its ictus is established
relative to *either* syllable that it stands next to. Clearly, this view
is an unusual one, but one that can be confirmed or refuted
empirically.

Since much of my analysis will appear more idiosyncratic than
it actually is, it is worth pointing out, as we go along, the similarities between what I try to do and what has been done by other
metrists. The idea that relative ictus is determined only between
adjacent units of the meter is stated well by Jespersen, from whom
I borrow a convenient notation.[5] A slanted line drawn between
two adjacent metrical units indicates the relative ictus of the two
units, so that iambic pentameter can be described as:

$$a \diagup b \diagdown a \diagup b \diagdown a \diagup b \diagdown a \diagup b \diagdown a \diagup b$$

Although Jespersen's system has the dubious virtue of abandoning
the traditional foot, it succeeds in expressing the concept of
intermediate metrical stress that I describe above—as in the following line that he cites from *Richard III* (p. 259):

$$1 \diagdown 2 \diagdown 3 \diagup 4$$
Grim-visag'd warre hath smooth'd his wrinkled front
(I.i.9)

The fact that I believe this scansion to be wrong for Shakespeare
and the reasons why will be discussed in Chapter Eight, below.
What is interesting is that the contour *can* be used to describe a
verse of Old English poetry:

$$1 \diagdown 2 \diagdown 3 \diagup 4$$

2285a   féasceaftum men;   frēa scēawode

By way of contrast, the second syllable of *féasceaft* in line 7 has secondary linguistic stress but no metrical stress at all, for it is not heavier than any adjacent syllable:

$$1 \searrow 2 \diagup 3 \searrow 4$$

$$\prime \quad x \quad \prime \quad x$$

7a   fēasceaft funden;   hē þæs frōfre gebād

As regards intermediate stress, it should be clear that I am interested only in the kind of pattern found in verse 2285a, for by the view that I shall continue to present, the secondary linguistic stress on *fēasceaft* in verse 7a has no metrical relevance.

The problem with theories that ignore intermediate stress is that they force one to dismiss several curious facts as accidents having no theoretical import. Type A verses with the following three characteristics have long been regarded as unmetrical, and none occur in *Beowulf*: those in which (i) the first thesis of the verse contains two syllables, (ii) the first of those syllables is long, and (iii) the three syllables of the first foot belong to a single word—schematically: $\perp \bar{x} x \mid \perp x$.[6] Stated as such, the structure may seem peculiar enough and its absence not particularly surprising. But many verses in *Beowulf* almost fit the description, lacking one or another of the characteristics. There are at least 650 verses that can be described as A verses with two syllables in the first thesis (Bliss's 1A1b and 1A*1a). Many of these have a long second syllable:

Bliss 1A1b $\prime \mid x \; x \quad \prime \quad x$
8a   wēox under wolcnum   weorðmyndum þāh

Bliss 1A1b $\prime \mid x \; x \; \prime\_x \; x$
580a   flōd æfter faroðe   on Finna land

Bliss 1A*1a $\prime \quad x \mid x \quad \prime \quad x$
856a   beornas on blancum.   Ðær wæs Bēowulfes

Bliss 1A*1a $\prime \quad x \mid x \quad \prime \quad x$
1148b   siþðan grimne gripe   Gūðlāf ond Ōslāf

There are at least sixty-five A verses (Bliss lists this many of his type 2A3a[ii], and some of his other patterns would count as well) in which the first foot consists of a three-syllable word. But in all of these the first syllable of the first thesis is short:

Bliss 2A3a   ´ ˘ ˘| ´ x
136a   morðbeala mãre,   ond nō mearn fore

Bliss 2A3a   ´   ˘ ˘| ´ x
156a   feorhbealo feorran,   fēa þingian

Bliss 2A3a   ´ ˘ ˘| ´ ˛x x
215a   gūðsearo geatolīc;   guman ūt scufon

If the second syllable in these lines were long, the structure in question would be fulfilled. But as it happens, type A verses do not begin this way. Another type does, however, and quite commonly; the most characteristic first foot of the E type consists of exactly the structure that does not occur in the A verse:

E   ´˛x ˋ   x| ´
93a   wlitebeorhtne wang,   swā wæter bebūgeð

E   ´ ˋ x| ´
110b   Metod for þȳ māne   mancynne fram

E   ´˛x ˋ x | ´
152b   hwīle wið Hrōþgār,   heteniðas wæg

E   ´ ˋ x | ´
719b   heardran hæle,   healðegnas fand

It is now possible to state the problem in somewhat simpler and more striking terms. The E verse never occurs with an extra unstressed syllable at the end, a fact that is most curious syntactically, for the missing pattern would be easy to construct; only a final inflectional syllable would have to be added to a pattern that occurs more than 400 times. It may seem at this point that I have created problems that do not exist, for if I am really talking about E verses, one might reason as follows: obviously there is no final inflectional syllable at the end, because E verses do not end that way. But labeling the verses "E" and dismissing them as such is simply giving a name to the problem and not explaining it. Type E does not differ from type A as bears differ from pigeons, where the absence of wings on one creature can be explained by citing its genus. As the examples above are intended to show, the two types have many elements in common. The interesting question is this: Which of these elements is it that crucially distinguishes type E so

that it cannot receive the unstressed syllable at the end? Bliss
offers an explanation in terms of the caesura (pp. 37–38), but since
the caesura as Bliss uses it is simply a syntactic boundary (which
in an E verse amounts to a word boundary), he has only stated the
problem in different terms, and the caesura itself becomes a fact
that requires explanation. I would claim that the crucial feature is
intermediate metrical stress.

Here again one must beware of confusing the linguistic concept
and the metrical. If it is obvious that verse 136a, *morðbeala māre*,
type A, has secondary linguistic stress on *-beal-*, it is not so
obvious that the syllable bears intermediate metrical ictus. The
syllable is short, and the overwhelming majority of intermediate
stresses in the second metrical position of the verse are long—or
resolved with the following syllable.[7] But if resolved stress is
placed on *-beal-* and *-a*, the metrical position fails to qualify for
intermediate metrical ictus, or indeed for any ictus at all, for
-beala does not have greater linguistic prominence than either of
the adjacent syllables, *morð-* or *mār-*:

<pre>
                      ′   ‵‿x   ′ x
136a   morðbeala māre,   ond nō mearn fore
</pre>

Thus, the abstract metrical pattern is ⊥ x x ⊥ x and not ⊥ ⊥ x ⊥ x.
Three levels of metrical stress in the first foot preclude the possibility of two levels of metrical stress in the second. To answer the
question originally posed, intermediate stress crucially distinguishes type E and certain subtypes of A.

Even if this line of reasoning fails to convince, there is an
independent argument for claiming intermediate stress in type E
verses, which involves the rather lengthy process of looking at the
individual lines and searching out parallels. Bliss finds four
subtypes of E without intermediate stress:

3E1	⊥ x x | ⊥
3E*1	⊥ x x | x ⊥
2E1a	⊥ x | x ⊥
2E1b	⊥ x | x x ⊥

He counts 118 occurrences in *Beowulf* of 3E1, 11 of 3E*1, 20 of
2E1a, and 2 of 2E1b. In what follows, I shall consider the 129

3E1 and 3E*1 verses together; in these the first three syllables occur in a single word. Then I shall comment briefly upon the 22 verses scanned as 2E1a and 2E1b.

Bliss marks the following two verses, in which the noun, *Bēowulf*, is inflected in the dative singular, as 3E1:

Bliss 3E1   ´   x x | ´
818b   burston bānlocan.   Bēowulfe wearð

Bliss 3E1   ´   x x | ´
2842b   būon on beorge.   Bīowulfe wearð

There is one E verse in which *Bēowulf* is inflected in the genitive singular:

Bliss 3E1   ´   x   x | ´
2807a   Bīowulfes biorh,   ðā ðe brentingas

In order to decide whether these readings are valid, one might ask whether there are verses in which the inflected noun, *Bēowulf*, must receive intermediate stress in order for the verse to be scanned properly. If one accepts the argument of Chapter Two—that all verses must have at least two metrical stresses—then in the following verses *Bēowulfes* must receive secondary linguistic stress, which counts as a metrical stress:

                                            x   x   ´   ⸜ x
856b   beornas on blancum.   Ðǣr wæs Bēowulfes

                 x x x   ´   ⸜ x
2194a   þæt hē on Bīowulfes   bearm ālegde

And there are eight instances in which the noun with the dative singular inflection must receive intermediate stress:[8]

                                            x x x x ´   ⸜ x
609b   brego Beorht-Dena;   gehȳrde on Bēowulfe

                 x   x   ´   ⸜ x
623a   þæt hīo Bēowulfe,   bēaghroden cwēn

                 x x   ´   ⸜ x
1043a   Ond ðā Bēowulfe   bēga gehwæþres

                 x x x x   ´   ⸜ x
1051a   þāra þe mid Bēowulfe   brimlāde tēah

```
           x   x   ′   ヽ  x
2207a      syððan Bēowulfe        brāde rīce

           x   x   ′   ヽ  x
2324a      þā wæs Bīowulfe        brōga gecȳðed

           x x   ′   ヽ  x
2907a      ofer Bīowulfe,      byre Wīhstānes

           x    x   ′   ヽ  x
3066a      Swā wæs Bīowulfe,       þā hē biorges weard
```

The same argument applies to the seven occurrences of inflected *Higelāc* that Bliss reads without intermediate stress. Verse 194b is typical:[9]

```
Bliss 3E1                                  ′‿x x x |  ′
194b            Þæt fram hām gefrægn       Higelāces þegn
```

There are four verses, however, in which intermediate stress on *-lāc-* must be assumed in order to have two stresses in the verse— 261a, for example:[10]

```
                 x     ′‿x ヽ  x
261a             ond Higelāces     heorðgenēatas
```

Bliss reads the two occurrences of *fēasceaftum* in *Beowulf* as 3E1:

```
Revised       ′    ヽ   x     ′
Bliss 3E1     ′    x   x  |   ′
2285a         fēasceaftum men;     frēa scēawode

Revised       ′    ヽ   x     ′
Bliss 3E1     ′    x   x  |   ′
2393a         fēasceaftum frēond;      folce gestēpte
```

Although this noun in the dative singular does not appear else-where, there is one occurrence of the nominative plural that makes the point just as well:

```
               x   x   x   ′   ヽ  x
2373a          Nō ðȳ ǣr fēasceafte       findan meahton
```

Inflected *ǣghwæðer* occurs twice in E verses:

```
Revised                              ′     ヽ   x    ′
Bliss 3E1                            ′     x   x |  ′
287b          ombeht unforht:      'Ǣghwæþres sceal
```

```
Revised                    ′    ＼  x        ′
Bliss 3E1                   ′    x  x  |    ′
2564b        ecgum unslāw;     æghwæðrum wæs
```

One of these forms also occurs in a C verse, where it must receive intermediate stress if the verse is to have two stresses:

```
                              x  x  ′    ＼   x
1636b        earfoðlīce     heora æghwæþrum
```

Similarly, the nominative singular form of *edwenden* occurs twice in contexts where Bliss reads it without intermediate stress:

```
Revised                    ′    ＼  x      ′
Bliss 3E1                   ′    x  x  |   ＼
1774b        Hwæt, mē þæs on ēþle     edwenden cwōm
```

```
Revised                    ′    ＼  x      ′
Bliss 3E1                   ′    x  x  |   ′
2188b        æðeling unfrom.     Edwenden cwōm
```

And it occurs once in a verse where intermediate stress would be required:

```
                        x  x  ′    ＼   x
280a         gyf him edwenden     æfre scolde
```

The adverb *semninga* occurs once in Bliss's 3E1 type and twice in contexts that would contradict that reading:

```
Revised                    ′    ＼  x  ′
Bliss 3E1                   ′    x  x|  ′
1767b        forsiteð ond forsworceð;     semninga bið
```

```
                        x    x  ′    ＼   x
644b         sigefolca swēg,     oþ þæt semninga
```

```
             x  x  ′    ＼   x
1640a        oþ ðæt semninga     tō sele cōmon
```

Similarly, the accusative singular form of *ǣnig*:[11]

```
Revised                    ′  ＼  x  ′
Bliss 3E1                   ′  x  x|  ′
3127b        syððan orwearde     ænigne dæl
```

```
             x  x  x  ′  ＼  x
627a         þæt hēo on ænigne     eorl gelȳfde
```

```
                              x  x  x  ′  ＼  x
1772b      æscum ond ecgum,      þæt ic mē ænigne
```

Although Bliss reads *Alwalda* without intermediate stress in verse 955b,

```
Revised                          ′  ＼  x  ′
Bliss 3E1                        ′  x  x |  ′
955b       āwa tō aldre.    Alwalda þec
```

he inconsistently reads it with intermediate stress in 1314a:

```
Bliss d2c      x  x  x  ′  ＼  x
1314a          hwæþer him Alwalda      æfre wille
```

and in 928b, he places secondary stress on *Alwealdan*:

```
Bliss 3E2                        ′  ＼  x |  ′
928b       ‘Ðisse ansȳne    Alwealdan þanc
```

The genitive singular form of *hlāford* in 3179a can be compared with the dative singular form in 2634b:

```
Revised        ′  ＼  x     ′‿x
Bliss 3E1      ′  x  x |    ′‿x
3179a          hlāfordes (hry)re,    heorðgenēatas

                                 x  x  ′  ＼  x
2634b          þonne wē gehēton    ūssum hlāforde
```

Inflected *æþeling* occurs seven times without intermediate stress by Bliss's reading. Verse 33b is representative:[12]

```
Revised                          ′‿x ＼  x   ′
Bliss 3E1                        ′‿x x   x |  ′
33b        īsig ond ūtfūs,    æþelinges fær
```

But the word also occurs eight times in verses where intermediate stress is necessary verses such as 3a:[13]

```
               x  x ′‿x ＼  x
3a             hū ðā æþelingas    ellen fremedon
```

Undyrne presents a curious situation, for it occurs twice in contexts where Bliss gives the second syllable no metrical stress:

Revised		′ ˋ x ′
Bliss 3E1		′ x x| ′
150b	ylda bearnum	undyrne cūð

Revised		′ ˋ x ′
Bliss 3E1		′ x x| ′
410b	on mīnre ēþeltyrf	undyrne cūð

and once where the second syllable would normally bear intermediate stress:

		x x ′ ˋ x
2911b	orleghwīle,	syððan under[ne]

and once where the second syllable must bear the alliteration.
Here Bliss and Pope quite rightly give -dyr- the heaviest stress in
the verse:

Pope A65	| ′ ˋ| ″ ˋ|
Bliss a1c	x x x ′ x
2000a	'þæt is undyrne, dryhten Higelāc

Unsōfte in line 2140 can be compared with *unsōfte* in line 1655:

Revised		′ ˋ x ′˳x
Bliss 3E1		′ x x | ′˳x
2140b	ēacnum ecgum;	unsōfte þonan

		x x ′ ˋ x
1655a	Ic þæt unsōfte	ealdre gedīgde

and *ungeāra* in 602b with *ungeāra* in 932a:

Revised		′ ˋ x ′
Bliss 3E1		′ x x | ′
602b	eafoð ond ellen	ungeāra nū

		x x ′ ˋ x
932a	Ðæt wæs ungeāra,	þæt ic ænigra mē

and the accusative singular form, *unfægne*, in 573a with the
nominative singular form, *unfæge*, in 2291a:

Revised	′ ˋ x ′
Bliss 3E1	′ x x| ′
573a	unfægne eorl, þonne his ellen dēah

```
          x    x  /  \ x
2291a     Swā mæg unfǣge    ēaðe gedīgan
```

Yrringa occurs in both an E verse and a C verse. The argument that I have been developing would require intermediate stress in each:

```
Revised                   /  \   x    /
Bliss 3E1                 / x   x |   /
1565b     aldres orwēna,   yrringa slōh
```

```
                          x x  /  \   x
2964b     Eafores ānne dōm.   Hyne yrringa
```

Īrenna occurs in both contexts with a double *n*:

```
Revised                   /  \   x    /
Bliss 3E1                 / x   x |   /
802b      ǣnig ofer eorþan   īrenna cyst
```

```
          x    x  /  \   x
2683a     þæt him īrenna    ecge mihton
```

The word also occurs twice with a single *n*:

```
Revised        /  \  x   /
Bliss 3E1      / x  x |  /
673a      īrena cyst    ombihtþegne
```

```
Revised        /  \  x   /
Bliss 3E1      / x  x |  /
1697a     īrena cyst    ǣrest wǣre
```

Klaeber states that *īrena* stands for the older form, *īrenna*.[14] That view is compatible with my own, since otherwise we would have to add two more occurrences to the rare group of verses with intermediate stress on a short syllable.

Singāle, singāla, and *singāles* in three verses that Bliss reads as 3E1 can be compared with *syngāles* in a C verse:

```
Revised       /   \ x   /_x
Bliss 3E1     /   x x |  /_x
154a      singāle sæce;    sibbe ne wolde
```

Revised   ′ ˋ x ′
Bliss 3E1   ′ x x | ′
190a   singāla sēað;   ne mihte snotor hæleð

Revised   ′ ˋ x   ′
Bliss 3E1   ′ x x | ′
1777b   ic þǣre sōcne   singāles wæg

                 x x ′ ˋ x
1135a   þā ðe syngāles   sēle bewitiað

And the genitive plural form, *gīganta*, can be compared with
the nominative plural, *gīgantas*:

Revised   ′ ˋ   x x ′
Bliss 3E*1   ′ x x| x ′
1562b   gōd ond geatolīc,   gīganta geweorc

Revised   ′ ˋ   x ′
Bliss 3E1   ′ x x | ′
1690b   gifen gēotende   gīganta cyn

                 x x ′ ˋ   x
113a   swylce gīgantas,   þā wið Gode wunnon

The present participles, *lifigende* (*lifigendum*), *slǣpendne* (*slǣp-ende*), *wæccende*, and *nīpende* occur in contexts where Bliss does
not assign intermediate stress and also in contexts where, by the
argument of Chapter One, intermediate stress is required:

Revised   ′‿x ˋ   x   ′
Bliss 3E1   ′‿x x   x | ′
1973b   lindgestealla   lifigende cwōm

Revised   ′‿x ˋ   x   ′
Bliss 3E1   ′‿x x   x | ′
1953b   līfgesceafta   lifigende brēac

Revised   ′‿x ˋ   x ′
Bliss 3E1   ′‿x x   x | ′
815a   lifigende lāð.   Līcsār gebād

                 x x ′‿x ˋ   x
2665b   þæt ðū ne ālǣte   be ðē lifigendum

Revised   ′ ˋ   x ′
Bliss 3E1   ′ x   x | ′
741a   slǣpendne rinc,   slāt unwearnum

Revised   ′ ＼   x   ′
Bliss 3E1   ′   x   x| ′
1581b   slōh on sweofote,   slǣpende frǣt

                 x   x   x   ′ ＼   x
2218a   þ(ēah) ð(e hē) slǣpende   besyre(d wur)de

Revised   ′ ＼   x   ′
Bliss 3E1   ′   x   x| ′
1268a   wæccendne wer   wīges bīdan

                x   x   ′ ＼   x
2841a   gif hē wæccende   weard onfunde

                x   x   ′ ＼   x
708a   ac hē wæccende   wrāþum on andan

Revised   ′ ＼   x   ′
Bliss 3E1   ′ x   x| ′
547a   nīpende niht,   ond norþanwind

                x   x   ′ ＼   x
649a   oþ ðe nīpende   niht ofer ealle

In addition to these present participles, there are six present participles in E verses without parallels in C verses:

Revised   ′ ＼   x   ′
Bliss 3E1   ′   x   x| ′
50a   murnende mōd.   Men ne cunnon

Revised   ′ ＼   x   ′
Bliss 3E1   ′   x   x| ′
159b   (ac se) ǣglǣca   ēhtende wæs

Revised   ′ ＼   x   ′
Bliss 3E1   ′   x   x| ′
2464a   weallinde wæg;   wihte ne meahte

Revised   ′ ＼   x   ′
Bliss 3E1   ′   x   x| ′
2832b   Nalles æfter lyfte   lācende hwearf

Revised   ′   ＼   x   ′
Bliss 3E1   ′   x   x| ′
3028b   Swā se secg hwata   secggende wæs

Revised   ′ ＼   x ′
Bliss 3E1   ′   x   x| ′
3145b   sweart ofer swioðole,   swōgende lēg

If we generalize from those present participles that have parallels in C verses to all present participles, then it could plausibly be argued that these verses, too, have intermediate stress—a view that accords, of course, with what the grammars report.[15]

Among the words which do not occur in decisive contexts are a number of compounds that the Wyatt-Chambers edition hyphenates, indicating that the semantic force of the two parts may justify an intermediate stress.[16] Verse 161b from that edition is typical:[17]

Revised		′ ＼ x ′
Bliss 3E1		′ x x| ′
161b	seomade ond syrede,	sin-nihte hēold

We have considered sixty-six of the verses that Bliss reads as 3E1 and 3E*1—without intermediate stress—and sixty-three remain. Of these, twenty-nine are inflected proper names, where it is plausible to assume intermediate stress.[18] Verse 455a, with *Wēlandes*, illustrates the group:[19]

Revised	′ ＼ x x ′	
Bliss 3E*1	′ x x	x ′	
455a	Wēlandes geweorc.	Gǣð ā wyrd swā hīo scel

For the remaining thirty-four verses,[20] I have no specific arguments except to point out that many of them have syntactic parallels in the verses that have already been discussed. Thus, beside *uncūðne* and *uncūþes*, we have *unfǣgne*, considered above:

Revised		′ ＼ x ′
Bliss 3E1		′ x x| ′
276b	ēaweð þurh egsan	uncūðne nīð
Revised		′ ＼ x ′‿x
Bliss 3E1		′ x x	′‿x
876b	ellendǣdum,	uncūþes fela
	′ ＼ x ′	
573a	unfǣgne eorl,	þonne his ellen dēah

And beside *gryrelīcne* and *longsumne*, adjectives in the accusative

case preceding a noun, we have *ǣnigne*, to which intermediate
stress has already been assigned:

Revised	$'$⌣x $\backslash$ x $'$	
Bliss 3E1	$'$⌣xx $x\,|\,'$	
1441a	gryrelīcne gist.	Gyrede hine Bēowulf

Revised	$'$ $\backslash$ x $'$	
Bliss 3E1	$'$ x $x\,|\,'$	
1536a	longsumne lof;	nā ymb his līf cearað

	$'$ $\backslash$ x $'$	
3127b	syððan orwearde	ǣnigne dǣl

In all of these E verses beginning with a trisyllabic word, it is
usually clear that three levels of linguistic stress are present; if the
preceding arguments have merit, it is also clear that all three
linguistic levels have metrical reality. More difficult, and less
common, are verses that might have three levels of metrical stress
in two, or even three, separate words. The syllable *-wulf-* in
2907a, *ofer Bīowulfe*, has secondary linguistic stress, and it
qualifies for intermediate metrical ictus, for it is more prominent
than *-e*; but the same syllable in 18a might or might not be more
prominent than the following *wæs*:

	$'$ $'$	
18a	Bēowulf wæs brēme	—blǣd wīde sprang—

And similarly, in 1024b, the relative prominence of *-wulf* and *ge-*
may not be obvious:

	$'$ $'$	
1024b	beforan beorn beran.	Bēowulf geþah

I would read 1024b with intermediate metrical stress on *-wulf* and
18a without it. Syntactic evidence can be found within the poem to
support these readings, but I have not assembled that evidence
and cannot insist upon my readings. I can state, however, my
working bias: given a choice of two plausible scansions, I would
tend to choose the pattern that is firmly established in unambiguous verses over a pattern that is anomalous. Pope reads verse 18a
and twelve other verses as type A* with intermediate stress:[21]

Pope A59	$|$ $\prime\prime$ $\backslash$ $|$ $\prime\prime$ $\backslash\,|$	
18a	Bēowulf wæs brēme	—blǣd wīde sprang—

He recognizes the possibility of *not* assigning intermediate stress in ten of these verses and suggests that the whole of type A* could be reduced to three verses. I find much merit in this suggestion, since $\perp$ x x $\perp$ x occurs unambiguously more than 700 times; and I would extend that reading to the other three verses as well (438a, 608a, and 1698a).

For verse 1024b, however, and for most of the other nineteen of Bliss's 2E1a, I would retain intermediate stress. In fifteen of the verses, the heavy second syllable of the compound or proper noun is compared with a light verbal prefix—*ge-*, *on-*, *ā-*, or *for-*, making a difference in linguistic prominence that seems sufficient to establish a difference in metrical ictus:

Revised		´ ` x ´
Bliss 2E1a		´ x | x ´
1024b	beforan beorn beran.	Bēowulf geþah

Two of the remaining verses, 747b, *ræhte ongēan*, and 2150a, *lissa gelong*, have traditionally been classified as deficient—a description that I would accept.[22] And two others, 881a and 954a, can be read as Pope reads them, as type A; so, too, can Bliss's two 2E1b patterns, 343b and 845a. Only the status of 1127b, *Hengest ðā gȳt*, remains uncertain in my mind.

The general point to make is that *some* differences in linguistic prominence are metrically significant and others are not. It is beyond the scope of this book to establish in detail the metrically significant differences, but several observations can be made. According to the condition argued for in Chapter Two, differences in metrical ictus depend upon differences in linguistic prominence, and differences in linguistic prominence depend, in turn, largely upon the syntactic structure. Thus, nouns and adjectives nearly always bear metrical ictus; prepositions and subordinating conjunctions seldom do; verbs and adverbs may or may not, depending upon their position in the phrase, the overall syntax, and the need for metrical ictus. The first part of this chapter argued that the second elements of compounds and certain other heavy syllables bear intermediate ictus when followed by a less prominent syllable—in verses that Bliss labels 3E1 and 3E*1. For those verses labeled 2E1a and 2E1b, it appears that the difference in prominence between the second element of compounds and syllables such as *ge-* is sufficient to establish metrical ictus—unlike the difference between *-wulf* and *wæs*, or *-gār* and *ond*, in verses labeled A*. This conclusion I would not insist upon until the various syntactic structures have been studied more extensively.

However, other conclusions can be stated firmly now. There are different ways of deciding that intermediate stress is an essential part of Old English meter. Chapter Two examined the problem of intermediate stress in verses that Bliss calls light *d1*, x (x) (x) (x) ⏜ x x, and concluded that the pattern was actually: x (x) (x) (x) ⏜ ⏜ x. Two arguments were used there. The first simply appealed to the grammars, finding that the classes of words to which secondary phonetic stress has traditionally been assigned were often the same classes that Bliss scanned without secondary phonetic stress (and consequently without intermediate metrical stress). To accept Bliss's scansion would require a radical revision of traditional rules of linguistic stress—rules deduced partly, but by no means wholly, from metrical considerations.

There was also a less obvious argument that could be made within the poem itself: the existence of verses such as *þǣr wæs Bēowulfes* and the absence of verses such as **þǣr wæs Bēowulf* permitted the inference of intermediate metrical stress in the former. Together with independent arguments concerning type A verses, this inference led to the conclusion that each verse of Old English had at least two metrical stresses, the important conclusion of Chapter Two.

That conclusion, in turn, permitted the more obvious of the two arguments advanced in the present chapter, where the problem was to show that type E verses must contain intermediate stress. If a word contains intermediate metrical stress in one context, it is plausible to assume that the same form of that word has intermediate metrical stress in another context; furthermore, it is not implausible to assume that the same word, inflected differently (genitive, for example, instead of accusative), has the same pattern of stress from one context to another. The possibility of three levels of stress in these words is important, for much of the previous discussion on the subject has aimed at excluding certain whole classes—even of inflected compounds—from the category of words that can receive intermediate stress.[23]

One can go further and say not only that it is possible to scan most of the words in Bliss's E patterns with intermediate stress, but also that certain unhappy consequences follow if they are not scanned that way. If one accepts $\perp$ x x (x) $\perp$ as a metrical pattern, one is faced with the fact that the pattern is filled almost invariably with words that are capable of bearing secondary linguistic stress and intermediate metrical ictus. There are only two exceptions in *Beowulf, lissa gelong* (2150a) and *ræhte ongēan* (747b). The alternative assumption—that the verses discussed in this chapter do have intermediate stress—is supported both by the arguments offered here and by analogy with numerous other verses. If the revised scansions are accepted, they fit a paradigm that describes hundreds of hemistichs where the pattern of stress is not in doubt, $\perp$ $\perp$ x (x) $\perp$, or Sievers' type E.

The less obvious argument of this chapter was the one presented first. I tried to show that intermediate stress crucially distinguishes type E from certain subtypes of A. The former type cannot have a final inflectional syllable because it contains three levels of stress in its first foot. Type A, in contrast, contains only two levels of stress that are metrically relevant and therefore permits a final unstressed syllable at the end.

NOTES

[1] Eduard Sievers, *Altgermanische Metrik* (Halle: Niemeyer, 1893), p. 26.

[2] Jakob Schipper, *A History of English Versification* (Oxford: Clarendon Press, 1910), p. 32. Actually, the difference between the two views is less than Schipper makes it appear, for Sievers is careful to distinguish between *schwächere Hebung* (as in the second foot of a C verse: x $\prime\prime$ | $\prime$ x, *Altgermanische*, pp. 27–28) and *Nebenhebung* (as in D and E verses). Sievers' conception of secondary stress seems to be exactly what Schipper states as his own, "an intermediate degree between the arsis and thesis, or strongly accented and unaccented member" (p. 32).

[3] A. J. Bliss, *The Metre of Beowulf*, 2nd ed. rev. (Oxford: Blackwell, 1967), p. 114.

[4] Samuel Jay Keyser, "Old English Prosody," *College English*, 30 (1969), 333, 346–48.

[5] See Otto Jespersen, "Notes on Metre," in *Linguistica: Selected Papers in English, French and German* (Copenhagen: Levin and Munksgaard, 1933), pp. 249–74.

6 See Henry Sweet, *An Anglo-Saxon Reader in Prose and Verse*, 9th ed. rev. C. T. Onions (Oxford: Clarendon Press, 1922), p. lxxxviii; and Bliss, *Metre*, pp. 3, 27, 37–38.

7 Klaeber—*Beowulf and the Fight at Finnsburg*, 3rd ed. (Boston: Heath, 1950), p. 279—lists, under "Rare Rhythmical Types," five type E verses in which unresolved short syllables occur in second position and bear intermediate metrical stress: 463b, 623b, 783b, 1584a, 2779b. Occasionally, D verses have unresolved short syllables in second position: Sievers counts thirteen of the pattern ⌐ | ⌣ ⌐ x. But the normal pattern is for secondary stress in second position to be long or resolved: in 755 type E verses, by Pope's count.

8 I should point out that there are at least two verses in *Beowulf* that would support an argument against secondary stress in the same terms that I am presenting my argument. One of these contains the genitive form, *Bēowulfes*:

		x x ′ x x ′
501b	onband beadurūne—	wæs him Bēowulfes sīð

For the other, see note 11, below. I have no explanation for either of these verses.

9 See also verses 1483b, 1574b, 1970b, 2169b, 2977b, and 2988b.

10 See also verses 342b, 407b, and 2943a.

11 Although with this compare 932b:

		x x ′ x x ′
932b	Ðæt wæs ungeāra,	þæt ic ænigra mē

12 See also verses 118b, 888a, 1408b, 1920b, 2597a, and 3170a.

13 See also verses 982a, 1244a, 1294a, 1596a, 1804a, 2374a, and 2888b.

14 Klaeber, *Beowulf*, p. 153n.

15 See A. Campbell, *Old English Grammar*, rev. ed. (Oxford: Clarendon Press, 1962), p. 34.

16 A. J. Wyatt and R. W. Chambers, eds., *Beowulf with the Finnsburg Fragment* (1914; rpt. Cambridge: Cambridge University Press, 1952).

17 See also verses 256a, 512a, 787a, 1271a, 1278a, 1416a, 1429a, 1513b, 1740b, 2182a, and 2890a.

18 For a discussion of the difference in stress between inflected and uninflected proper names in *Beowulf*, see Winfred P. Lehmann, "Metrical Evidence for Old English Suprasegmentals," *Texas Studies in Language and Literature*, 1 (1959), 66–72.

19 See also verses 19b, 455a, 499b, 829a, 877a, 884b, 1009b, 1066b, 1089b, 1091a, 1199b, 1492b, 1538a, 1612b, 1931b, 1944b, 1961b, 2037b, 2357b, 2379a, 2387b, 2392b, 2482b, 2501b, 2551a, 2602b, 2611b, and 3076b.

20 Verses 130b, 179a, 207b, 276b, 429b, 876b, 891a, 899b, 1072b, 1158a, 1269b, 1379a, 1441a, 1536a, 1582b, 1584a, 1657b, 1760b, 1822b, 1959b, 1972b, 2115b, 2268b, 2337b, 2406b, 2447a, 2695a, 2789b, 2817b, 2882b, 2938b, 2979b, 3038b, 3075a. Verse 838b is apparently listed incorrectly.

21 See John C. Pope, *The Rhythm of Beowulf*, 2nd ed. rev. (New Haven: Yale University Press, 1966), pp. 263, 332. Verses 61a, 308a, 438a, 608a, 780a, 1017a, 1148b, 1189a, 1649a, 1698a, 2434a, and 2602a.

22 Ibid., pp. 320, 372.

23 See Bliss, *Metre*, pp. 24–26; see also Keyser, "Old English Prosody," pp. 346–48.

FIVE

Clashing Stress in Types C and D

A conspicuous feature of Old English meter that accounts for much of its strangeness to the modern reader is the frequent occurrence of clashing stress. Especially in half-lines traditionally scanned as type C or D, the effect of two consecutive stresses is quite different from the characteristic effect of iambic meter in Modern English. In both C and D verses, the two main stresses occur back to back, sometimes in compound nouns, sometimes in phrases: verse 383a of *Beowulf, tō West-Denum*, is type C; verse 235a, *þegn Hrōðgāres*, type D. There is good reason to believe that the heaviest stress of most Old English compounds fell, as in Modern English, upon the first syllable.[1] The pattern of stress in Old English phrases, however, presents something of a problem that bears directly upon any theory of Old English prosody.

For those phrases spoken without emphatic or contrastive intonation, the phonological rules of Modern English can assign stress quite predictably. A well-known pattern, which recently has been formulated in transformational phonology as the nuclear stress rule, may be stated informally, and somewhat imprecisely, as follows: the heaviest stress in English phrases occurs most neutrally upon the last heavy stress of the phrase, so that we characteristically say *bláck bírd*, or *demánd capitulátion*, or *the mán who came to dínner*, rather than *bláck bírd*, or *demánd capitulá-tion*, or *the mán who came to dínner*.[2] Since, as speakers of Modern English, we retain this rule on those occasions when we read Old

65

English poetry, many of us, perhaps most of us, read *bād bolgen-
mōd*, or *wīs wēlþungen*, with heavier stress on the second of the
two adjacent, stressed syllables. Certainly some of our best and
most sensitive recordings of Old English poetry reflect this
characteristic pattern of Modern English.[3] The evidence that I shall
present below, however, suggests that the most natural reading
for us was not the proper reading from the point of view of the
Anglo-Saxons; specifically, one may deduce from several independent arguments that the eighth-century *scop* intended for the
first, not the second, of two clashing stresses to be more prominent.
The effect is quite different from that which most of us would
intuitively produce in our reading of several hundred verses in the
Beowulf.

To be sure, it matters little in the familiar systems of Old English
meter which of the two clashing stresses is heavier. In Sievers' type
D1 (́⁻ | ́⁻ ́⁻ x) the first syllable could theoretically always be
heavier than the second, or always lighter, or indifferently heavier
or lighter. The important point is that the two syllables be the
heaviest in their respective feet. Since comparisons in Sievers'
system are made within, but not between, feet, the question of
which main stress is phonetically heavier does not arise.

Throughout this discussion I shall continue to distinguish
between phonetic, or linguistic, stress and metrical stress. A
proper metrical description makes use only of the linguistic
facts necessary for describing the meter. According to Sievers, the
pattern of phonetic stress in *Hrōðgāres* is metrically relevant and
should be included in an account of the meter, but the phonetic
pattern of the whole verse, *þegn Hrōðgāres*, whether ⁻ ⁻ ⁻ x, or
⁻ ⁻ ⁻ x, has no relevance for prosody. Thus, in Sievers' metrical
pattern ⁻ | ⁻ ⁻ x, the relative phonetic stress of the first two
syllables is systematically obscured. If it can be shown that
Sievers' type D1 is, phonetically, always of the form ⁻ ⁻ ⁻ x,
then it may be a defect of his metrical theory that the theory does
not express this fact. The theories of Bliss and, to some extent, of

Pope would suffer the same defect; in practice, the most natural intonation for the modern reader would quite clearly be wrong. In fact, there are three pieces of objective evidence in support of this (for us) unnatural reading, and a fourth, somewhat impressionistic, observation. I shall confine my attention to the most relevant types—those that Sievers labels C (basically, x $\perp$ | $\perp$ x) and D (basically, $\perp$ | $\perp$ $\perp$ x and $\perp$ | $\perp$ x $\perp$).

(i) Alliteration. Of the 853 D verses by Pope's count, the 505 with single alliteration all alliterate on the first stress. Of the 1,118 C verses, only 78 have double or crossed alliteration, and the rest alliterate without exception in the first foot.[4] C and D verses do not alliterate on the second stress alone.

Although stress, and not alliteration, is the basic element of Old English meter, alliteration is the most obvious clue to the pattern of stress. If one or both of two consecutive syllables within a verse can alliterate, but when only one does it is always the same one, then it is logical to assume that the stressed syllable which never alliterates alone is the less strongly stressed of the two.

(ii) Compounds. There are many C verses in which the first stress is necessarily greater, for it is the first syllable of a compound word:

```
C                    x    ′   ‵  x
243a         mid scipherge      sceðþan ne meahte
```

In the majority of C verses, especially of the first half-line, the two main stresses occur within a single word, often a compound. Of the twenty-two examples of Pope's C1, first half-line, the two clashing stresses in all but three occur within a word, where the first stress is characteristically heavier.[5] If one assumes that this phonetic pattern extends to the three verses where the clashing stresses occur in separate words (an assumption which seems plausible, if the verses are really of the same metrical type, but not necessary, if one begins by assuming Sievers' feet), then verse 2264a can be read as Pope reads it, with heaviest stress on *sæl* (p. 288):

```
Pope C1     | (,)  ‵  |  ″    ‵    |
2264a          geond sæl swingeð,     nē se swifta mearh
```

The pattern is different from the most usual pronunciation of Modern English, where we would stress more heavily the latter of the two words, whichever it might be: *flíes through the háll, through the háll flíes.*

The same line of reasoning applies to verses of type D. If the grammars are correct in reporting main stress on the first syllable of compounds and of most other words, there are many verses with four descending degrees of phonetic stress:

	′ ^ ˋ x
245a	lindhæbbende, nē gē lēafnesword
	′ ^ ˋ x
246a	gūðfremmendra gearwe ne wisson
	′ ^ ˋ x
377b	Ðonne sægdon þæt sǣliþende
	′ ^ ˋ x
464b	ofer ȳða gewealc, Ār-Scyldinga

Again, an analysis such as Sievers' would have no use for the patterns sketched here, for it would claim that the difference in stress between *lind-* and *hæb-*, though real phonetically, is of no metrical import. For the moment, however, I am interested only in establishing the linguistic facts, which can, of course, be discussed with reference to no system of meter, since the meter is a second level of abstraction. If we assume that verses composed of a single word have a phonetic pattern that is shared also by certain similar verses composed of more than one word, then we could describe verse 229b as follows:

		′ ^ ˋ x
229b	Þā of wealle geseah	weard Scildinga

This, too, is different from the most neutral intonation of Modern English, where we would say: *the guârd of the Scíldings*, or *the Scîldings' guárd*.

It is, of course, possible to argue that the nuclear stress rule applies in Old English poetry as it does in Modern English, and that D verses characteristically have two different phonetic shapes—one for compounds and one for phrases:

```
            ′    ʌ ʽ   x
1019a       Þēod-Scyldingas      þenden fremedon

                             ʌ    ′ ʽ   x
229b        Þā of wealle geseah      weard Scildinga
```

These patterns would have no metrical significance, since the relevant fact is that two stresses clash initially, and it does not matter which of the two is heavier. Division into Sievers' feet would then rightly obscure the phonetic difference:

```
D           ′   |   ′ ʽ  x
1019a       Þēod-Scyldingas      þenden fremedon

                             ′   |   ′ ʽ   x
229b        Þā of wealle geseah      weard Scildinga
```

Although this is the traditional analysis, and consistent within itself, I find it unconvincing. The two possible ways of reading verse 229b are so different that I must conceive of the first as being metrically similar to verse 1019a and the second as being similar in terms of metrical stress (though violating the rules of alliteration) to verse 274a:

```
                             ′    ʌ ʽ  x
229b        Þā of wealle geseah      weard Scildinga

                             ʌ    ′ ʽ  x
229b        Þā of wealle geseah      weard Scildinga
D           ′  |  ′  ʽ  x
1019a       Þēod-Scyldingas      þenden fremedon
C           x   x   ′  |  ʽ   x
274a        þæt mid Scyldingum      sceaðona ic nāt hwylc
```

(iii) Syllabic quantity. By Pope's count, 504 of the 1,118 C verses in *Beowulf* have a short, unresolved syllable for the second arsis, while the first arsis is always long (pp. 288–300, 348–57):

```
                        x   ′   |  ᵕ x
253b        lēasscēaweras      on land Dena

                        x   ′   |  ᵕ x
509b        ond for dolgilpe      on dēop wæter
```

<pre>
               x ′ | ˘ x
</pre>
1340a   gē feor hafað   fǣhðe gestǣled

<pre>
                       x ′ | ˘ x
</pre>
2656b   Wedra ðēodnes.   Ic wāt geare

There are no verses of the form:

<pre>
               x ˘ | ˎ x
                * tō cyninge
</pre>

Given a long stressed syllable and a short stressed syllable in
juxtaposition, one cannot simply assume that the long syllable is
the more heavily stressed of the two. But since length is concomi-
tant with stress throughout Old English meter, the facts given here
are suggestive and worth consideration.

In type D, both of the two major stresses are usually long, but
in the small group of verses where one is short and unresolved, it is
always the second:

<pre>
              ′ | ˘ ˎ x
</pre>
2a   þēodcyninga   þrym gefrūnon

<pre>
              ′ | ˘ ˎ   x
</pre>
46b   ǣnne ofer ȳðe   umborwesende

<pre>
               ′ | ˘ ˎ x
</pre>
258b   Him se yldesta   andswarode

<pre>
               ′ | ˘ ˎ x
</pre>
340b   Him þā ellenrōf   andswarode

<pre>
               ′ | ˘ ˎ   x
</pre>
372b   Ic hine cūðe   cnihtwesende

<pre>
                ′ | ˘ ˎ   x
</pre>
535b   Wit þæt gecwǣdon   cnihtwesende

<pre>
                ′ | ˘ ˎ   x
</pre>
1004b   ac gesēcan sceal   sāwlberendra

<pre>
                 ′ | ˘ ˎ x
</pre>
1039b   þæt wæs hildesetl   hēahcyninges

<pre>
                ′ | ˘ ˎ x
</pre>
1155b   eal ingesteald   eorðcyninges

<pre>
                       ′ | ˘   ˎ x
</pre>
1210b   Gehwearf þā in Francna fæþm   feorh cyninges
</pre>

		´‿x |ᵕ ` x
1684b	on geweald gehwearf	woroldcyninga

		´| ᵕ ` x
2382b	þone sēlestan	sæcyninga

		´ |ᵕ ` x
2503b	nalles hē ðā frætwe	Frēscyning[e]

		´ |ᵕ ` x
2694b	Ðā ic æt þearfe [gefrægn]	þēodcyninges

		´ | ᵕ ` x
2912b	Froncum ond Frȳsum	fyll cyninges

		´‿x |ᵕ ` x
3180b	cwǣdon þæt hē wǣre	wyruldcyning[a]

(iv) Among those scholars whose intuitions on these matters are keenest, several see a tendency, if not a rule, for the first arsis of C and D verses to be more heavily stressed. In discussing clashing stress in C and D types, Tolkien speaks of the necessity of reducing the second stress. The order of his numbering, one should remember, is the reverse of that currently used in linguistics: "To a full *lift* a value 4 may be given. The *subordinate stresses* (reduced in force and lowered in tone) that appear in such compounds as *highcrèsted* may be given value 2. But reduction also occurs in other cases. For instance, the second of two clashing stresses in a sentence; or of two juxtaposed words (of equal significance when separate), such as nouns and adjectives, tends to be reduced to approximate value 3."[6] Tolkien's statement is admirable for its clarity and precision, as indeed is his whole essay, but his restraint and understatement suggest that he is repeating an obvious fact that requires no supporting evidence (and for which none is given). The fact which he states, however, is really quite remarkable when its implications are drawn out, as I try to do below, and in any case his analysis is not obvious to such skillful readers as Pope and Bessinger, who fail to read many of the lines as Tolkien describes them.

Although Sievers is not as explicit as Tolkien about type D, he does believe that the first stress is usually the heavier, and with regard to type C, he is quite definite: "Die beiden hebungen sind im vortrag nicht notwendig gleich stark. . . . So dominiert beim zusammentreffen zweier haupthebungen im typus C x ⌣ | ⌣ x . . . sichtlich die erste über die zweite . . . so dass man das versschema geradezu auch als x ⌣ | ⌣ x bezeichnen kann."[7] Again, this information is presented as a somewhat redundant fact about the verse, as though it were predictable from other features within the basic metrical system, or from the structure of the language itself.

Against the facts of alliteration, word stress, and the intuitions of some (but not all) of our best scholars, there is the solid objection that the analysis offered here seems unnatural to the modern reader. Such an objection is more than the straw man it might seem, for it entails one of two situations, neither of which is immediately plausible: either the rule for nuclear stress is an innovation, a rule added to the language, since *Beowulf*, or the metrical patterns of Old English often contradicted the patterns of ordinary speech. If the second alternative is the case, then Sievers' traditional division of the verse into feet is called into question; we would need instead an abstract metrical pattern that specified heavier phonetic stress upon the first of all clashing stresses, contrary to the most neutral patterns of intonation. If the first alternative is the case, then Sievers' system can stand as it is, but we must radically revise our view of the history of English stress.

Either task would be a formidable one, but one or the other would logically follow from the arguments presented above. Of the two possibilities, a reconsideration of Sievers' feet would be the less ambitious and more promising effort, and reconsiderations of the sort have, of course, been offered from time to time. Pope, though concerned with temporal values rather than stress, arrives at an unorthodox view of the D verses that is, I believe, in many ways parallel to the view of the present study. He finds it necessary to read *wīs wēlþungen* with extra length upon *wīs*. In musical notation Pope marks the temporal value ♩ | ♪ ♪ ♪, but as regards stress, he often follows the natural pattern of Modern English, reading ⌃ ⌣ ⌣ x. In light of the evidence presented above, I would be happier with a reading in which the pattern of stress was always ⌣ ⌃ ⌣ x, and the temporal pattern, following predictably, would be the pattern that he gives. One could then use the line of reasoning to justify both extra stress and extra length on *wīs* that Pope presents in support of extra length. The most neutral patterns of ordinary speech are not, by Pope's view, necessarily the patterns of heroic poetry: "Admittedly this reading is somewhat artificial. It belongs to formal declamation, where a relatively high value tends to be set on logical clarity and rhythmic order. . . . The rhythm I give to *wīs wēlþungen* and similar verses sounds right to me because what it lacks in familiarity it makes up for in clarity of expression."[8]

To say that the first of two clashing stresses in Old English verse takes heavier stress is, in a large number of cases, to say the obvious; many verses must be read in that way, particularly those with both stresses in a compound word, or else we do violence to our intuitions and to well-established views of Germanic stress. The verses that do not so readily lend themselves to such a reading are those verses that consist of phrases, where it is natural for us to stress most heavily the last of the heavy stresses in the phrase. I have tried to suggest, however, that the effect of unemphatic phrasal stress is so very different from the effect of stress within compound words that it is hard to justify grouping the two types into a single metrical class. The evidence of alliteration and syllabic quantity indicates that we should redefine those types with clashing stress, stating explicity that the first of two consecutive stresses must always be the heavier. By this approach, Sievers' types C and D would apply to the same verses as before, but the definitions of the patterns would contain information that had been supplied neither by the original metrical description nor by the rules of the language. This information would require, in many verses, a pattern of intonation strikingly different from the pattern that the modern reader would normally give.

NOTES

[1] See A. Campbell, *Old English Grammar*, rev. ed. (Oxford: Clarendon Press, 1962), pp. 30–33.

[2] See Noam Chomsky and Morris Halle, *The Sound Pattern of English* (New York: Harper and Row, 1968), pp. 15–24, 89–91. More precisely, as Chomsky and Halle

point out, this description applies to Modern *American* English. Modern British English has level stress in adjective plus noun combinations. The general point is the same, for the Modern British pattern, too, is unlike the Old English pattern.

3 For example, John C. Pope's reading of *Selections from Beowulf* (Pleasantville, N.Y.: Educational Audio Visual, Inc.), verses 28b, 208b, 214a, 216b, 218a, 748b, 761b, and many others; and Jess B. Bessinger, Jr.'s reading of the same lines with the same pattern of stress on *Beowulf, Caedmon's Hymn and Other Old English Poems* (New York: Caedmon Records, Inc., 1962).

4 See John C. Pope, *The Rhythm of Beowulf*, 2nd ed. rev. (New Haven: Yale University Press, 1966), pp. 288–314, 348–66.

5 Ibid., p. 288.

6 In John R. Clark Hall, trans., *Beowulf and the Finnesburg Fragment*, 3rd ed. rev. C. L. Wrenn; "Prefatory Remarks" by J. R. R. Tolkien (London: Allen and Unwin, 1950), p. xxx, n. 2. See also p. xxxvi: "In all patterns the first lift is as a rule (for phonetic and syntactic reasons) the stronger. This is always the case in C, Da and b, and E. These patterns must bear the stave [alliteration] on the first lift or both (not only on the second lift)."

7 Eduard Sievers, *Altgermanische Metrik* (Halle: Niemeyer, 1893), p. 27.

8 Pope, *Rhythm*, p. xx.

SIX

Metrical Simplicity and Type D

The present chapter attempts to reclassify two minor subtypes of the basic Five Types, and at the same time to suggest a method of simplifying Sievers' description as a whole in a fundamental way. By the view presented here, patterns D2 and E should be regarded as a single metrical type: for example, verse 709a of *Beowulf*, *bād bolgenmōd*, which Sievers designates D2 (´ | ´ x ´), should be classed metrically with verse 50a, *murnende mōd*, Sievers' E (´ ´ x | ´), instead of with 613a, *cwēn Hrōðgāres*, Sievers' D1 (´ | ´ ´ x). While the division into the subtypes D1 and D2 clearly captures certain features that verses of these patterns have in common, I shall argue that these features are syntactic rather than metric and that there are deeper metrical similarities between types D2 and E. This conclusion leads to a reconsideration of the expanded subtype D* and its relation to the normal type D. In Sievers' system, verses such as *Beowulf* 223a, *sīde sǣnæssas*, are described as D* (´ x | ´ ´ x), with five *Glieder*, or metrical units, instead of the normal four. But by Max Kaluza's view, this fact points to a striking asymmetry in Sievers' scheme: all of the types and subtypes describe *viergliedrige Verse*, except for the one subtype D*, which is a *fünfgliedriger* pattern.[1] The discussion of types D2 and E below offers a possible clue to the solution of this inconsistency.

The present analysis rests partly upon an assumption argued above—that the first of two clashing stresses in types C and D is always more prominent.[2] If this is the case, then Sievers' two variants of D can be represented abstractly as follows:

$$\text{D1} \qquad 1 \diagdown 2 \diagdown 3 \diagdown 4$$
$$\text{D2} \qquad 1 \diagdown 2 \diagdown 3 \diagup 4$$

The numbers represent *Glieder*, or metrical positions, not syllables (for a position may be filled by more than one syllable; a resolved arsis, for example, consists of a short stressed syllable and the following syllable). The lines between the numbers trace the contour of stress, a notational device suggested by Jespersen's analysis of Modern English verse. At this level of abstraction, the motivation for collapsing types D2 and E into a single pattern is clear, for E is identical to D2:

$$\text{E} \qquad 1 \diagdown 2 \diagdown 3 \diagup 4$$

To be sure, Sievers had reasons for considering types D1 and D2 together, for the two patterns share a number of features. I would argue, however, that the obvious similarities between D1 and D2 result from the ways in which the patterns are realized, especially as regards word boundaries, and that these superficial similarities, while of great interest for stylistic purposes, are less important metrically than are the deeper correspondences between D2 and E. Specifically, D1 and D2 alliterate on one or both of the first two syllables, while E alliterates on the first syllable, or the first and the last. But the first stress of type D1 or D2 usually falls on a monosyllabic word, or a disyllabic word with a short first syllable, which is thus resolved; the first stress of what we call type E usually falls on the first syllable of a trisyllabic or polysyllabic word, often a compound. The differences in alliteration that result from these realizations of the abstract patterns are quite predictable: since there are relatively few compounds in Old English with the same initial sound in both parts, one would not expect an E verse to alliterate on the first two stresses. If one recognizes that an E verse characteristically consists of a trisyllable or polysyllable plus a monosyllable, while a D verse, either D1 or D2, characteristically consists of a monosyllable plus a trisyllable or a polysyllable, then many of the similarities between D1 and D2 and many of the differences between D2 and E result predictably from these syntactic realizations of the abstract pattern rather than from the abstract pattern itself.

That this observation is in some measure true can be seen by examining D and E verses that are not realized in the usual way. It is not at all obvious in the following verses that Sievers' D1 and D2 patterns form one distinct type, or that his E pattern forms another. Sievers somewhat hesitantly scans the verses as E; Pope, also hesitantly, scans them as D:[3]

Pope D18		∥(ˏ) ∥ ∖
Sievers E		′ ˏ x ′
871b	sōðe gebunden;	secg eft ongan

Pope D18		∥(ˏ) ∥ ∖
Sievers E		′ ˏ x ′
1146b	Swylce ferhðfrecan	Fin eft begeat

Pope D18		∥ (ˏ) ∥ ∖
Sievers E		′ ˏ x ′
1526b	hondgemōta,	helm oft gescær

Pope D18		∥ (ˏ) ∥ ∖
Sievers E		′ ˏ x ′
1615b	since fāge;	sweord ær gemealt

Pope D18		∥(ˏ) ∥ ∖
Sievers E		′ ˏ x ′
2570b	tō gescipe scyndan.	Scyld wēl gebearg

Pope D18		∥(ˏ) ∥ ∖
Sievers E		′ ˏ x ′
2777b	bēacna beorhtost.	Bill ær gescōd

Pope D19		∥‿(ˏ) ∥ ∖
Sievers E		′‿x ˏ x ′
123b	þrītig þegna;	þanon eft gewāt

Pope D19		∥‿(ˏ) ∥ ∖
Sievers E		′‿x ˏ x ′
171b	mōdes brecða.	Monig oft gesæt

There are more than sixty other verses quite similar to these (Pope's D16–19, second half-line), including eleven that Pope originally read as D verses, but changed in his 1966 edition to a scansion with three main stresses (p. xxiii). Representative are:

Pope 1966		*"* ‿(ˑ) *"* *"*
Pope 1942		*"* ‿(ˑ) *"* ˎ
121b	grim ond grǣdig,	gearo sōna wæs
Pope 1966		*"* (ˑ) *"* *"*
Pope 1942		*"* (ˑ) *"* ˎ
745b	fēt ond folma.	Forð nēar ætstōp
Pope 1966		*"* (ˑ) *"* *"*
Pope 1942		*"* (ˑ) *"* ˎ
897b	Wælses eafera;	wyrm hāt gemealt
Pope 1966		*"* (ˑ) *"* *"*
Pope 1942		*"* (ˑ) *"* ˎ
2073b	glād ofer grundas,	gǣst yrre cwōm

In all of these verses, and many like them, a slight shift in stress changes the metrical category from D to E, or even from one of these two-stress patterns to a dubious three-stress pattern. Such a small change in pronunciation seems more a phonetic detail than a fact about the meter. In each case, however, the contour of stress as I have described it is unambiguously 1 ╲ 2 ╲ 3 ╱ 4.

This scansion has the advantage of revealing similarities in the second part of D2 and E verses that are not shared with type D1. At the same time, it claims that D2 and E are metrically identical— a claim that is not obvious—and it ignores similarities in the first two positions of D1 and D2. A better description of the three types might be as follows (where the symbol △ indicates longer duration):

D1 795a	1 ╲ 2 ╲ 3 ╲ 4 △ ˊ △ ˊ ˎ x eorl Bēowulfes
D2 998a	1 ╲ 2 ╲ 3 ╱ 4 △ ˊ △ ˊ x ˎ eal inneweard
E 528a	1 ╲ 2 ╲ 3 ╱ 4 ˊ ˎ x ˊ nihtlongne fyrst

Pope would mark *eorl* and *eal* with half-notes, *niht-* with a quarter-note.

The reality of the extra length that we feel in reading the two D verses is attested by experiments in Modern English that measure the acoustic and articulatory correlates of phonetic prominence in structures similar to these. Philip Lieberman found that increased temporal quantity occurs predictably whenever extra emphasis is assigned to phonological segments. For example, the prominence upon words given contrastive stress results from their being marked [+emphatic]. Instead of the usual level of prominence assigned by the stress rules, emphatically marked segments receive longer duration, increased loudness, and higher pitch.[4] The problem in applying these findings to Old English, of course, is the uncertainty of whether the relevant rules of stress have changed.[5] For purposes of the present argument, I shall make what seems to be the more cautious and conservative assumption—that the rule of phrasal stress in Old English operated in normal speech much as it does in Modern English, throwing heaviest stress to the end of the phrase, to the right, instead of to the left as in compounds[6] (but see note 7, below).

The main conclusion of Chapter Five (that the first of two clashing stresses in Old English poetry was more prominent) would require that the most neutral pattern of phrasal stress be overridden by the meter. The first of two consecutive stresses would have to receive metrical ictus in addition to the prominence assigned by the normal operation of the stress rules. In the most neutral pattern of intonation for Modern English, verse 795a would have primary stress on *Bēo-* and secondary stress on *eorl*, in accordance with the phrasal stress rule:

$$\wedge \quad \prime \quad \grave{} \quad x$$
eorl Bēowulfes

As a verse of Old English poetry, however, the relative stress would be just the reverse:

$$\prime \quad \wedge \quad \grave{} \quad x$$
eorl Bēowulfes

One may assume that the word *eorl* is given extra prominence because of the meter. If Lieberman's data for Modern English can be applied to Old English, extra temporal length would be expected:[7]

′ △ ∧ ＼ x
eorl Bēowulfes

This analysis suggests the solution to the puzzling D* verses, the only *fünfgliedrige* types in Old English. In place of the dummy symbol for time that the regular D verses have, the D* type fills the position with an unstressed syllable:

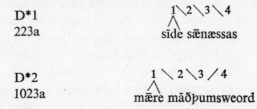

D*1   1＼2＼3＼4
223a   sīde sǣnæssas

D*2   1 ＼ 2＼3 ／ 4
1023a   mǣre māðþumsweord

Kaluza was right in sensing that the extra syllable makes little alteration in the rhythm,[8] but the present analysis (which amounts to resolution of a long syllable) tries to show the relation between this rhythm and others. A variety of structures in Old English poetry count as long syllables and thus qualify for metrical stress. A syllable is long if it contains a long vowel:

                              ′
507a   on sīdne sǣ

or contains a short vowel, if the syllable is closed by a consonant:

                              ′
30a   þenden wordum wēold

or contains a short vowel in an open syllable if the syllable is resolved with a following syllable:

                         ′‿x
129a   micel morgenswēg

And a short, unresolved syllable can receive stress in certain contexts, the most common of which is the penultimate syllable of a C or D verse:

                             ◡
103a   mǣre mearcstapa

To say that a long syllable can be "resolved" in a specific environment complicates an already complex rule only slightly, and it lends an overall symmetry that makes suspension of resolution more plausible than some critics have found it. If it is true, as Sievers has argued, that greater ictus resides in the first part of the verse than in the last, then the usual syllabic length plus an extra measure in *mǣre* would help give that *Glied* more ictus than *mearc-*, which in turn would have more ictus than unresolved *sta-*, which would be heavier than *-pa*:

103a   mǣre mearcstapa

Stress on long syllables is the norm, but at the end of a verse a short syllable can take stress, and at the beginning, in those verses where three stresses of varying degrees occur, the first long syllable can receive additional length. This view is supported by the absence of expanded E verses, where a long syllable would have to be resolved at the end, without the reasons that can be given for the expanded D verses:

$$
\begin{array}{cccc}
1 & 2 & 3 & 4 \\
\end{array}
$$

*sǣnæssas sīde

Although I have dealt in this chapter with only two of the Five Types, the implications bear directly upon the other three types and upon the system of meter as a whole. It is the D type, in its subtype D*, that confounds an exceedingly simple statement of the metrical paradigm, for D* is the only subtype with five *Glieder* instead of the normal four. If the second syllable of subtype D* can be included in the first metrical unit for reasons of temporal quantity that I have presented above, then Sievers' statement of the metrical pattern can be turned upside down. Instead of enumerating the Five Types, which multiply to as many as 130,[9] one can state the general principle that produces the various types: a verse must consist of exactly four *Glieder*.

Certain constraints, such as the one argued in Chapter Five (that the first of two clashing stresses is heavier) together with more familiar requirements concerning vowel quantity, resolution, alliteration, and the like, would serve to define the *Glieder* of the general statement—to describe exactly how the four abstract entities are realized as syllables. These constraints, like the general principle, are in the form of statements, which can be formalized as rules. This kind of description is quite unlike an enumeration of the various patterns, for it attempts to express the principles by which the patterns are produced. Chapter Seven will consider the logical relationship between a single pattern of four *Glieder* and Sievers' Five Types.

NOTES

1 Max Kaluza, *Englische Metrik in historischer Entwicklung dargestellt* (Berlin: Felber, 1909), pp. 42–43; trans. A. C. Dunstan, *A Short History of English Versification* (London: Allen, 1911), p. 46. Kaluza disregards the rare (and dubious) A* pattern (see above, pp. 60–61). For a half dozen verses read with the dubious E* pattern, see John C. Pope, *The Rhythm of Beowulf*, 2nd ed. rev. (New Haven: Yale University Press, 1966), pp. 318, 371. Since all of these can more plausibly be scanned with four positions, I shall follow Kaluza in considering only D* verses as possible exceptions to the four-member system.

2 See Chapter Five, pp. 65–73, above.

3 Eduard Sievers, "Zur Rhythmik des germanischen Alliterationsverses I," *Beiträge zur Geschichte der deutschen Sprache und Literatur*, 10 (1885), 257–58; and Pope, *Rhythm*, pp. 363–64.

4 See Philip Lieberman, *Intonation, Perception, and Language*, Research Monograph No. 38 (Cambridge, Mass.: MIT Press, 1967), pp. 75, 88–89, 144–47.

5 On this question, and for more on prominence in Old English, see two studies by Robert D. Stevick, *Suprasegmentals, Meter, and the Manuscript of Beowulf* (The Hague: Mouton, 1968), pp. 24–25, 36; and *English and its History: The Evolution of a Language* (Boston: Allyn and Bacon, 1968), pp. 291–96.

6 See Noam Chomsky and Morris Halle, *The Sound Pattern of English* (New York: Harper and Row, 1968), pp. 15–24, 89–91.

7 Henry Sweet states, without supplying evidence, that *gōd mann* in normal speech was stressed *gŏd mann*; see *A New English Grammar* (Oxford: Clarendon Press, 1900), I, 243, 889ff. I find this view, unorthodox as it is, quite attractive, especially as regards the argument of Chapter Five, above. Such a view would require a restatement of the present argument (since extra duration in the first arsis could not be explained as a result of extraordinary stress assignment). Lieberman has found increased duration or "disjuncture" to occur in careful speech in Modern English at word boundaries separating two heavily stressed syllables (*Intonation*, pp. 149–59).

He suggests that patterns of disjuncture correspond closely to the constituent structure of certain kinds of phrases (including potential type D patterns such as *light house-keeper*). This fact could partly account for the difference in temporal pulse between *eal inneweard* and *nihtlongne fyrst*.

8 Kaluza, *Englische Metrik*, pp. 84–85; *Short History*, pp. 90–91.

9 See A. J. Bliss, *The Metre of Beowulf*, 2nd ed. rev. (Oxford: Blackwell, 1967) pp. 123–27.

SEVEN

The Abstract Pattern of Old English Meter

The first chapter of this study stated Sievers' paradigm of Old English meter and considered briefly certain theoretical implications of his approach and of others. Subsequent chapters have examined details of Old English prosody and proposed revisions of Sievers' scheme or, in some cases, a return to his analysis from refinements and modifications that have been made during this century. In themselves, none of the points that I have argued changes radically our view of Old English verse. Now, however, I wish to return to a theoretical perspective and consider whether the various revisions, each of which can be motivated on independent grounds, are consistent among themselves. The framework within which we might discover that consistency was hinted at in the conclusion of the preceding chapter.

What is vaguely disturbing about Sievers' system has less to do with the kind of details that we have examined than with the Five Types themselves. The obvious question to ask is why Old English meter should consist of exactly the patterns that Sievers presents and no others. Recall that the Five Types, as Sievers described them, are really six:

A	´ x | ´ x
B	x ´ | x ´
C	x ´ | ´ x
D1	´ | ´ ` x
D2	´ | ´ x `
E	´ ` x | ´

Old English prosody allows all of these and yet excludes a pattern such as:

$$* \acute{} \grave{} \text{ x } | \acute{} \text{ x}$$

One might reasonably ask why.

We can sharpen the import of the question by reference to current linguistics, where the rationale for asking *why* has evoked elaborate and explicit metatheory. Chomsky distinguishes three levels of adequacy in linguistic description: from lowest to highest, *observational adequacy*, *descriptive adequacy*, and *explanatory adequacy*.[1] It is not condescending to say that Sievers' model attains the goal of observational adequacy by accounting in detail for many facts, nor presumptuous to suggest that by approaching those facts from a different direction we might see how to raise the model to a higher level of adequacy. We can appreciate the inclusiveness of Sievers' work and at the same time question its plausibility as a paradigm of meter.

The present chapter offers a hypothesis that purports to explain why Old English verse has just the patterns that it has. The explanation that I propose is on an abstract and logical level— what I have called a descriptive level. To the higher question of why these patterns should have psychological or aesthetic reality, I shall sketch some tentative answers in the final chapter. Here I shall limit the claims, none too modestly, to the level of descriptive adequacy. For theoretical and expository purposes, the analysis will focus upon the differences between my system and Sievers'. Then I shall try to show the similarities and suggest that there are relationships as well between both of these views and certain competing theories of the nineteenth century.

The most important claim that I wish to make is that *Beowulf* can be scanned with four metrical positions to the verse. By the interpretation of position implied in the earlier chapters of this study, we count not only the main metrical stresses but also the intermediate stresses, if there are any, and the metrically unstressed sequences, of which there are often two and always at least one. In types A and B, and most verses of type E, four positions are usually obvious:

$$1\diagdown 2\diagup 3\diagdown 4$$

A   ´ x ´ x
10b   ofer hronrāde   hȳran scolde

$$1\diagup 2\diagdown 3\diagup 4$$
$$\diagup\!\diagdown$$

B   x x ´   x   ´
277b   hȳnðu ond hrāfyl.   Ic þæs Hrōðgār mæg

$$1\diagdown 2\diagdown 3\diagup 4$$

E   ´   ᷉   x ´
542a   flōdȳþum feor   flēotan meahte

Although some A patterns (and D patterns as well) appear to have
five positions because of an extra unstressed syllable, or anacrusis,
at the beginning, we have seen that the syllables of the anacrusis
are subject to constraints that do not apply to other syllables of
the verse.[2] I have argued that the anacrusis of type A (and presumably also of type D) should not count as a regular position.
This view is identical with that of Sievers, though not with some
later interpretations of his system. Verse 217a of *Beowulf* would
have, then, the normal four positions:

                     ´   ´
217a   Gewāt þā ofer wǣgholm   winde gefȳsed

In types C and D, two stresses always occur consecutively.
Since they occur within separate feet, there is no mechanism in
Sievers' system to account for their relative stress:

C   x ͟ | ͟ x
D1   ͟ | ͟ ͜ x
D2   ͟ | ͟ x ͟

Chapter Five adduced several independent arguments—having to
do with alliteration, syllabic quantity, and the pattern of stress in
compound words—to support the claim that the first of two clashing stresses in types C and D is always more prominent. In
accordance with this view, I would read the following verses with
a heavier first stress:

	1 / 2 \ 3 \ 4	
C	x ′ ′ x	
4a	Oft Scyld Scēfing	sceaþena þrēatum

	1 \ 2 \ 3 \ 4	
D1	′ ′ \ x	
164b	Swā fela fyrena	fēond mancynnes

	1 \ 2\3 / 4	
D2	′ ′ x \	
709a	bād bolgenmōd	beadwa geþinges

The only problem with scanning C and D verses this way is the subtype that Sievers called D*, a pattern with apparently five metrical positions instead of the normal four. Verse 223a is typical:

	′ x ′ \ x	
223a	sīde sǽnæssas;	þā wæs sund liden

The unstressed syllable in *sīde* is the troublesome one, which I have accounted for in terms of temporal resolution.[3] With reference to acoustical experiments in Modern English, I tried to show that the extra unstressed syllable is not an anomaly but a perfectly predictable feature of phonological structures such as these. If the syllable does not occur, its place is filled by a pause or by extra vocalic length upon the preceding syllable. In short, the two syllables of *sīde* count as a single metrical position by the scansion that I propose—a scansion by no means conventional though similar to the reading that Kaluza described many years ago, relying mainly upon his keen intuitions.[4]

A final point must be made before I attempt a statement of Old English meter. Although type D2 ends on a secondary stress ($\angle$ | $\angle$ x $\angle$) and type E on a full stress ($\angle$ $\angle$ x | $\angle$), it should be clear that this difference in degree of linguistic stress has no bearing upon the meter as the meter is here conceived. The principle of relative stress between adjacent units leads us to remark only that the final unit in each type is heavier than the penultimate unit—that the contour of stress between the last two units is a rising contour, whether the pattern of phonetic stress is x $\angle$, x $\wedge$, or x $\angle$.

Altogether, I am able to find five contours that emerge from conditions that I would impose, for independent reasons, upon the meter. My five contours correspond roughly to Sievers' five types: A and B are the same as his; C, D, and E are somewhat different because of clashing stress and the fact that I group D2 with E:

A	1 \ 2 / 3 \ 4
B	1 / 2 \ 3 / 4
C	1 / 2 \ 3 \ 4
D1	1 \ 2 \ 3 \ 4
D2, E	1 \ 2 \ 3 / 4

The very interesting point to make is that these patterns are not random but inevitable. An examination of logical possibilities reveals the following fact: given four units, between any two of which the level of stress must rise or fall, there are eight possible patterns:

(1)	1 \ 2 / 3 \ 4
(2)	1 / 2 \ 3 / 4
(3)	1 / 2 \ 3 \ 4
(4)	1 \ 2 \ 3 \ 4
(5)	1 \ 2 \ 3 / 4
(6)	1 / 2 / 3 \ 4
(7)	1 / 2 / 3 / 4
(8)	1 \ 2 / 3 / 4

Patterns express the proportions holding between adjacent units, and proportions must be either ascending or descending. Four units permit three proportions. Since a proportion must take one of two forms, there are 2^3, or eight, possibilities. The first five of these are the patterns listed in the preceding paragraph. The last three are patterns in which the second of two clashing stresses is heavier. According to the view assumed here, these patterns with clashing stress were prohibited in Old English poetry.

The implications of this exercise are worth spelling out. If all of the verses in *Beowulf* can be described by one of the five patterns sketched above, then the constraints upon the permitted sequences of metrical positions can be stated more directly than they have been stated in the past. Instead of positing five completely different

The Abstract Pattern of Old English Meter   89

kinds of feet: (1) $\acute{-}$ x, (2) x $\acute{-}$, (3) $\acute{-}$, (4) $\acute{-}$ $\acute{-}$ x, (5) $\acute{-}$ x $\acute{-}$, which occur arbitrarily in eight combinations (1 + 1, 2 + 2, 2 + 1, 3 + 4, 3 + 5, 1 + 4, 1 + 5, 4 + 3), one can simply say that a verse has four metrical positions that may occur in any combination, with the condition that the second of two clashing stresses cannot be heavier. This would explain why Old English poetry has exactly five types, rather than four, or six, or three.

It would also explain why each kind of foot can occur in just the combinations that it can—why an A foot, $\acute{-}$ x, for example, can follow a B foot, x $\acute{-}$, to give a C verse, x $\acute{-}$ | $\acute{-}$ x, but why it cannot precede it: *$\acute{-}$ x | x $\acute{-}$. On the assumption that Sievers' feet express the equalities of the verse, there is no explanation that I can see for the extreme rarity of the pattern *$\acute{-}$ x | x $\acute{-}$ (and no justification for our suspicions of the two occurrences in *Beowulf*). And there is no explanation for the absence of $\acute{-}$ x $\acute{-}$ plus $\acute{-}$, or $\acute{-}$ $\acute{-}$ x plus $\acute{-}$ $\acute{-}$ x, or $\acute{-}$ x plus $\acute{-}$, or any of the other combinations of feet that do not occur.

To be sure, there are patterns missing from *Beowulf* that the system proposed here does not discuss. In each case, however, one must ask whether it is the task of the metrical system to make the mechanism of exclusion explicit—whether the absence of the pattern might not follow naturally from features of the linguistic system or from some other extra-metrical consideration. It may appear to be a fact about the meter, for example, that the number of unstressed syllables in a thesis depends upon the position of the thesis. Type A never has more than one unstressed syllable in the second thesis, though it may have as many as four in the first thesis:

A   ′ x x x x ′ x
435a   ic þæt þonne forhicge,   swā mē Higelāc sīe

A   ′ x   x ′ x
3062b   gewrecen wrāðlīce.   Wundur hwār þonne

The explanation for the different number of syllables in the two positions might well be in the system of linguistic stress, and if so, that explanation should not be stated in the metrics. The pattern $\acute{-}$ x $\acute{-}$ x x might be an unnatural one to realize syntactically:

indeed, the last three syllables could hardly occur in a single word, for one of the syllables would have secondary stress, which would count in the meter as intermediate stress—as in 3062a above:

$\prime$ $\grave{}$ x
wrāðlīce. Nor could the last three syllables be filled by monosyllabic or disyllabic nouns or adjectives, for nouns and adjectives cannot occupy theses. And even particles would not do very well, because the phrasal stress rule would throw stress to the right, giving prominence to normally unstressed words at the end of the phrase: *þonne* is unstressed medially in 435a above, but stressed finally in 3062a. Moreover, it is always unsatisfactory to have a string of weakly stressed monosyllables at the end of the verse because of the uncertainty of the pattern: Pope suggests that *hwār* might be more prominent than *þonne* in the verse above, and the pattern type D instead of A.[5] A similar kind of uncertainty attaches to the strings of monosyllables in verses scanned as E* (see Pope, p. 371).

All of this is not to suggest that the pattern $\perp$ x $\perp$ x x was impossible in Old English, but that its absence seems not especially surprising. If the absence can, in fact, be explained as a natural result of the linguistic system, then it would be inappropriate for the metrical system to burden itself with additional rules; for though it is important that the meter state the essential constraints, it is equally important that the meter make no more statements than are necessary.

Although I have emphasized the differences between my system and Sievers', the results are not as far apart as the initial assumptions. In effect, I have shuttled a few of the subtypes from one category to another, collapsed two classifications, and performed other minor changes. I believe that the implications of a four-unit system are more extensive than I have suggested, but speculations upon this matter must be saved for the final chapter. At this point, it can be said with certainty that there are indeed five types of verse in Old English, and they look very much like the five types that Sievers proposed. What Sievers did not explain was what these patterns, with their strangely dissimilar feet, have in common—and also why one could not, in principle, add a sixth or a seventh type, or take one away. I have tried to show that the five types are not the meter itself but the inevitable result of the meter, which is a four-unit pattern.

Even here Sievers, though he failed to ask the obvious question, presented the key to the answer by including in his system a concept that has since been generally ignored. In addition to describing a verse as containing two feet, Sievers described feet as containing one, two, or three *Glieder*. Quite frequently the *Glieder* correspond to what I have been calling metrical positions. By Sievers' view, the great majority of verses consist of four *Glieder* and are called *viergliedrige Verse*; the remaining verses, mostly type D*, consist of five *Glieder* and are called *fünfgliedrige Verse*.[6] If *Glieder* could occur in any combination, then the meter as Sievers conceived it could be described by saying that a verse consists of four or five *Glieder*; but since *Glieder* cannot so occur, a statement of the meter must contain some constraint. Sievers states the constraint by grouping the *Glieder* into sequences, which he calls "feet," and his system permits only certain combinations of these feet, two feet to the verse.

Partly because of the terminology, and partly because the feet of A, B, and C verses resemble the feet of classical and modern prosody, subsequent interpretations of Sievers' system have generally ignored his basic unit and have concentrated upon the groupings of those units into feet, which often have a linguistic reality, for they correspond more closely to syntactic divisions than the *Glieder* do. In a study such as Bliss's, the foot boundaries become syntactic boundaries, and the concept of meter as a measure of equalities is altogether lost. It is possible by Bliss's view to have "light" verses containing only one stress and no foot boundary, and a pattern such as x x x _⸜_ x becomes as acceptable as _⸜_ x | _⸜_ x. What I have tried to do in this chapter is to state directly the constraints upon the possible sequences of *Glieder* without introducing the intermediate unit of the foot. The result is a simplification of the whole system and a partial explanation of otherwise curious facts.

Interestingly, the present theory also establishes continuity with another tradition of prosodical investigation. During the latter part of the nineteenth century, the idea of a four-unit meter was vigorously pursued, only to be abandoned and forgotten after Sievers' theory gained general acceptance. Karl Lachmann was the first to scan Germanic poetry with four metrical beats, as early as 1831, and he was followed by E. Jessen, Arthur Amelung, Bernhard ten Brink, and Moritz Trautmann.[7] Kaluza made the important change of counting *Glieder* (stressed and unstressed members) instead of *Hebungen* (stressed members only), but he rightly considered his theory a part of the four-beat tradition.[8] In failing to define adequately the *Glieder* of his system, however, Kaluza was forced to list the acceptable patterns one by one. Since his list ran to ninety patterns, it is understandable why Sievers' apparently simpler Five Types prevailed.

Of the problems that remained unresolved after Sievers' theory appeared, perhaps the most perplexing is the one that Kaluza recognized and which I have tried to treat above: the general failure to see that the two-beat theorists and the four-beat theorists were often stating the same facts, though they were looking at the facts from opposite ends of the instrument. There is no contradiction in recognizing five types on the one hand, and four beats, or *Glieder*, or units, or positions, or members, or whatever one wishes to call the equalities of the verse, on the other—if one understands that the five types (slightly redefined, I would argue, from Sievers' scheme) are the linguistic realizations of the four metrical units. If one accepts the traditional rules of Old English prosody, modified by several constraints that I have observed, then four metrical units necessarily produce five patterns—no more than five, and no fewer.

NOTES

[1] Noam Chomsky, "Current Issues in Linguistic Theory," in *The Structure of Language*, ed. Jerry A. Fodor and Jerrold J. Katz (Englewood Cliffs, N.J.: Prentice-Hall, 1964), pp. 62–63. Chomsky's procedure, to be sure, is not peculiar to linguistics. See Thomas S. Kuhn, *The Structure of Scientific Revolutions* (Chicago: University of Chicago Press, 1962), p. 33: "These three classes of problems—determination of significant fact, matching of facts with theory, and articulation of theory—exhaust, I think, the literature of normal science, both empirical and theoretical."

[2] See Chapter Three, pp. 32–37, above.

[3] See Chapter Six, pp. 80–81, above.

[4] Max Kaluza, *Englische Metrik in historischer Entwicklung dargestellt* (Berlin: Felber, 1909), pp. 84–85; trans. A. C. Dunstan, *A Short History of English Versification* (London: Allen, 1911), pp. 90–91.

[5] John C. Pope, *The Rhythm of Beowulf*, 2nd ed. rev. (New Haven: Yale University Press, 1966), p. 327.

[6] Eduard Sievers, *Altgermanische Metrik* (Halle: Niemeyer, 1893), pp. 25–35.

[7] See Karl Lachmann, "Über althochdeutsche Betonung und Verskunst" and "Über das Hildebrandslied," in *Kleinere Schriften zur deutschen Philologie*, Vol. I of *Kleinere Schriften*, ed. Karl Müllenhoff (Berlin: Reimer, 1876), pp. 358–406, 407–48; E. Jessen, "Grundzüge der altgermanischen Metrik," *Zeitschrift für deutsche Philologie*, 2 (1870), 114–47; Arthur Amelung, "Beiträge zur deutschen Metrik," *Zeitschrift für deutsche Philologie*, 3 (1871), 253–305; Bernhard ten Brink, "Altenglische Literatur," in *Grundriss der germanischen Philologie*, Vol. II, pt. 1, ed. Hermann Paul (Strassburg: Trübner, 1893), 510–50; and Moritz Trautmann, "Die neueste Beowulfausgabe und die altenglische Verslehre," *Bonner Beiträge zur Anglistik*, 17 (1905), 175–91.

[8] Kaluza, *Englische Metrik*, pp. 69–100; *Short History*, pp. 74–107.

EIGHT

The Melody of *Beowulf*

The preceding seven chapters have presented a number of separate arguments and a synthesis. The discussion as a whole amounts to what may reasonably be called a theory of Old English meter. If the arguments are original, the conclusions that they support are not. Virtually every major conclusion of this book has been stated by at least one reputable scholar—often by more than one, and sometimes in refutation of a contrary idea held by another reputable scholar. Some claims, then, will be more plausible at first blush than others, depending upon the reader and the points of view that he brings with him. But each claim has its independent justification, arrived at inductively through an examination of the text.

Chapter Seven tried to show that these various claims, which often have no apparent relation to each other, fall together in support of a single principle of meter that has hitherto been overlooked or stated imperfectly. Unlike the independent arguments supporting the single principle, the discovery of the principle itself, so far as I am aware, is an original discovery. The principle, again, is this: given four metrical positions and certain constraints upon those positions, a model of meter will produce exactly eight contours:

$$(1) \quad 1 \searprow 2 \nearrow 3 \searrow 4$$
$$(2) \quad 1 \nearrow 2 \searrow 3 \nearrow 4$$
$$(3) \quad 1 \nearrow 2 \searrow 3 \searrow 4$$
$$(4) \quad 1 \searrow 2 \searrow 3 \searrow 4$$

(5) $1 \setminus 2 \setminus 3 / 4$
(6) $1 / 2 / 3 \setminus 4$
(7) $1 / 2 / 3 / 4$
(8) $1 \setminus 2 / 3 / 4$

The first five of these were permitted in Old English poetry; the last three were excluded.

It is perhaps appropriate to repeat one metatheoretical comment upon the process of investigation that I have followed. The difference between the separate statements of Chapters Two through Six and the single principle revealed in Chapter Seven is the difference between two levels of adequacy in metrical description—what Chomsky would call the difference between "observational adequacy" and "descriptive adequacy," or what Thomas S. Kuhn describes as the difference between "determination of significant fact" and "matching of facts with theory." There is still a third goal in grammar and in science—the level of "explanatory adequacy," in Chomsky's terms, or the "articulation of theory" in Kuhn's. Something analogous may be imagined as the final goal of this inquiry into prosody.

What remains to be done is to interpret the quasi-mathematical synthesis of Chapter Seven so as to explain the aesthetic and psychological reality that such a model might have. I have drawn upon scholarship in musicology and linguistic intonation, two areas of research that often draw in turn upon the results of metrical study. This final chapter tries to suggest two interpretations of the abstract metrical pattern, one theoretical, the other historical. The first, the theoretical interpretation, argues that a faulty assumption underlies almost all serious work in Old English meter, including the present study: the assumption that linguistic stress can distinguish three degrees of metrical ictus. Sievers' types D and E require three levels of stress; Pope, though his theory is rhythmic, assumes the reality of Sievers' levels; my own theory, if I may presume, requires not just three levels but four. I shall argue that neither stress nor quantity alone could make the distinctions necessary in Old English poetry—that the main correlate of metrical ictus was relative pitch, and not simply the pitch of ordinary discourse, but a heightened and stylized pattern.

The historical interpretation grows directly out of the theoretical. I shall suggest that the metrical basis of Old English poetry was the melodic formula, a contour of pitch drawn from a set of five contours out of a possible set of eight, to which words were fitted according to strict rules. We will look briefly at the melodic structures of religious chant and of secular forms such as the *chansons de geste* to indicate the extent of composition by melodic formula during the early Middle Ages and to suggest the possibility of a similar principle of composition for Old English poetry. Here recent speculations upon the use of the harp are especially interesting.

The five patterns that I have posited for Old English poetry, using numbers to represent positions and slanted lines to indicate the relation of each position to its neighbor, can be described by an equivalent graphic device of dots placed at different levels. Since the remaining discussion will mainly be concerned with the full contours of the five patterns, it will help to use that device:

A	$1\diagdown2\diagup3\diagdown4$	
B	$1\diagup2\diagdown3\diagup4$	
C	$1\diagup2\diagdown3\diagdown4$	
D	$1\diagdown2\diagdown3\diagdown4$	
E	$1\diagdown2\diagdown3\diagup4$	

On the basis of arguments presented in earlier chapters of this book, I am prepared to defend these patterns. If one does not accept them, then one must accept what I consider to be intolerable consequences: if type E, for example, does not require three levels of metrical ictus, then one is hard pressed to explain the conspicuous absence of verses such as *lissa gelong*. Several years ago, when I began my investigations into the Old English verse-form, I tried to simplify Sievers' patterns and reject what struck me as superfluous complications—the inclusion of syllabic length, for example, and of intermediate stress. The simplified patterns, partly resembling those proposed by Keyser, Baum, and others who have

attempted to solve the Anglo-Saxon puzzle, led to the consequences that I have mentioned and forced a return to patterns
resembling those of the more careful metrists Sievers and Pope
(to the extent that Pope uses and refines upon Sievers' system). My
type D differs from Sievers' in having four levels of metrical ictus
instead of three; and my type C differs in always having three levels
of ictus instead of sometimes having two. The point to note is the
need in both my system and Sievers' for at least one level of intermediate stress. While I am willing to believe logically in three or
four levels of metrical ictus, I am unable for aesthetic, psychological, and acoustic reasons to accept more than two.

It would be rather different if I were writing twenty years ago,
when American linguistic theory described four degrees of phonemic stress in Modern English.[1] I could then advertise my own
discoveries as confirmation of a parallel system in Old English.
Unfortunately, four degrees of phonemic stress have fared poorly
in the laboratory and in the classroom, when measured by instru-
ments and by skeptical ears.[2] Some of the most interesting experimental work on the subject has been done by Philip Lieberman,
whose terminology I shall borrow to keep straight at least half a
dozen concepts.[3] *Duration, fundamental frequency*, and *amplitude*,
as Lieberman defines the terms, are the acoustic correlates of
linguistic *prominence*. *Fundamental frequency* and *pitch* are inter-
changeable in his usage and in mine; *amplitude*, an acoustic
correlate, corresponds to the articulatory correlate *intensity*.[4]
Stress, by Lieberman's view, is a different concept still—the
abstract pattern produced in generative phonology by operation
of the stress cycle. Chomsky and Halle compute at least eight
levels of stress in the sentence, "My friends can't help being
shocked at anyone who would fail to consider his sad plight."[5] I
shall designate this mentalistic pattern *generative stress* to distinguish it from *phonemic stress*, which in Trager-Smith phonology
occurs on four levels. The difference between the two views is more
than the mere number of levels: Chomsky and Halle are careful
not to claim, as the structuralists do, that the levels of generative
stress are distinguished acoustically; they argue that the ideal
pattern of stress, as computed internally from knowledge of the

syntactic surface structure, need not have detailed physical reality.[6] Whether or not either kind of stress has acoustic correlates is an empirical question, subject to experimental verification.

Several investigators have found that for pairs of two-syllable words such as *rebél* (v.) and *rébel* (n.), the stressed syllables are, in fact, distinguished by acoustic correlates of higher fundamental frequency, increased amplitude, and longer duration.[7] But when one turns from binary distinctions in two-syllable words to intermediate levels of stress, the correspondences fail to hold. Lieberman states the problem by asking questions that apply directly to our patterns of Old English verse:

Can "degrees" of prominence differentiate intermediate levels of stress? Can a listener compute some sort of "prominence" function from the fundamental frequency, amplitude, and duration of each vowel, and differentiate stress level 1 [the highest level] from stress level 2 and further differentiate stress level 2 from stress level 3? The results of a number of independent psychoacoustic experiments suggest that listeners can make only binary categorical distinctions along the dimension of prominence when they listen to connected discourse.[8]

Lieberman finds that acoustic and physiologic correlates fail to correspond to stress, not only in connected discourse but in isolated phrases as well. In the ubiquitous *light housekeeper*, a good candidate for a C or a D verse, the peak fundamental frequency and peak amplitude of *house* and *keep* were the same in one recording, although *house* has stress level 1 and *keep* stress level 3 (pp. 151–52). (The only relevant acoustic cue in the recorded phrase was the extra duration between the syllables *light* and *house* to distinguish it from *lighthouse keeper*; Lieberman found that even this cue disappears in unambiguous phrases.)

If one rejects, as one must, four levels of phonemic stress and the physical reality of generative stress, then one must perforce have second thoughts about the patterns of Old English meter that we have arrived at inductively. Even if my patterns are found to be unacceptable for reasons I have not anticipated, the same problems attach to Sievers' types D and E and the same questions must be answered. Lest it seem that I have trusted overmuch to instrumental analysis, I should emphasize that the most convincing argument against four levels of phonemic stress is not the demonstration of their lack of physical reality, but the demonstration that linguists trained in Trager-Smith methodology fail to agree in their transcriptions. It is not likely that one would find closer agreement upon such matters in the mead-hall. I should add that the various acoustic experiments simply confirmed my own doubts about intermediate levels of ictus. It was never clear to me why Jespersen could argue for intermediate metrical stress in Modern English lines such as the one he cites from *Richard III*:[9]

> 1 ╲ 2 ╲ 3 ╱ 4
> ′   ╲   x   ′
> Grim-visag'd warre hath smooth'd his wrinkled front
>   (I.i.9)

The contour, which resembles Old English type E, surely has some kind of *linguistic* reality (as ideal stress if nothing else), but to my ear it is *metrically* the same as Pope's:

> ′   x   x   ′
> Mark how it mounts, to Man's imperial race
>   (*Essay on Man* I.209)

Metrically, a binary contrast between ictus and non-ictus, no matter what the several kinds of linguistic description might be. This is essentially what Wimsatt and Beardsley argue in their persuasive essay—that there are two levels of metrical ictus in Modern English, Trager-Smith phonemic levels to the contrary notwithstanding.[10] The same problem occurs in Old English verse. Three levels of *metrical* stress in *Hrōþgāres scop* fail to register in my brain, even though a simple survey of patterns in the text tells me that three levels must be there.

In all candor, I would take fewer pains to demonstrate the inadequacy of my system did I not believe solutions to be ultimately forthcoming. In particular, I believe something can be learned from looking at certain problems in musicology that overlap, for obvious reasons, though more than one might expect, the problems of the metrist. Those problems overlap especially in the borderland between speech and song—the area of intonation or speech-melody (from the metrist's point of view), or of recitative (from the musicologist's). Sievers understood the importance of speech-melody in his later work and inspired several studies to be undertaken within his theory of *Schallanalyse*.[11] Recent advances in phonological research put us in a more favorable position than Sievers, whose later work has not enjoyed the wide acceptance of the Five Types that he himself repudiated.

Recitative, as defined by Apel, is "a vocal style designed to imitate and emphasize the natural inflections of speech. . . . In the recitative, the purely musical principles of vocal melody, phrase, and rhythm are largely disregarded, being replaced by speechlike reiteration of the same note, slight inflections, irregular rhythms, purely syllabic treatment of the text, etc."[12] J. Smits van Waesberghe draws a continuum between speech and song with a misty borderland between the two containing various kinds of recitative. The less melodic recitatives are closer to speech, imitating, in stylized form, normal intonation.[13] As a general rule, according to Smits van Waesberghe, the more a recitative becomes music, the further the enunciation will deviate from speech.

Although recitative is most familiar to us as an element of modern opera, it has a much earlier (and discontinuous) history in medieval times as an element of monophonic music. The psalmody of Gregorian chant is the largest and finest body of such music in Western culture. A similar body of music is missing for secular texts, but contemporary accounts and a few fragments allow speculation. Musicologists often assert, perhaps too confidently, that the common roots of European epic extend to a period when verse was fitted to melodic formulas and chanted to recognizable melodies. Smits van Waesberghe views the various melodic patterns of Gregorian chant as "musical crystallizations" of patterns occurring in normal speech. He ascribes a similar technique to the singers of secular compositions, including those of most interest to us: the forms of recitative furthest from music are not

found in the musical repertory of Europe after 1600, but in the religious music and the national epics of those peoples whose evolution has not reached the stage of what we call modern culture. There was a time when European culture also cultivated these forms, not only in the national epics of the Germans mentioned by Tacitus, in the Carolingian *carmina gestatoria*, in the *Chansons de Geste* performed as recitatives, but also in early Christian religious music, which is still performed, among which the Gregorian Psalmody occupies a first place.[14]

Evidence for the technique of composing and performing early epic, scant as it is, can be deduced from two or three extant melodies to which *chansons de geste* may have been sung and from the often-cited observation of Johannes de Grocheo, who, writing about 1300, explained that each line of the *chanson de geste* was sung to the same tune.[15] If we find the aesthetics of such a technique bewildering in the twentieth century, it is well to remember that their ears had different expectations from ours. Or, as J. A. Westrup explains: "These fragments are very short, and modern taste might find it intolerable to hear a long poem recited to a constant repetition. The listener's interest, however, would be directed to the narrative, not to the tune to which it was sung. The music serves a practical purpose; at the same time it has something of the character of primitive incantation, a form of magic which survives still in the repeated supplications of the litany."[16] Friedrich Gennrich makes the relationship between the music of the *chanson de geste* and litany even more explicit, classifying the secular form in terms of the sacred.[17]

Before proceeding to consider medieval music, it is well to forestall criticism by anticipating it and reminding ourselves of what we are trying to do. One may accept the proposition that Old English poetry was sung and yet consider this, the setting of the text to music, a separate problem from the problem of meter, as in Modern English song. But it is conceivable that the two problems are inseparable—that a description of the meter is impossible without a consideration of the melody. I have tried to explain why I believe that ordinary linguistic categories are incapable of explaining types C, D, and E in Old English: simply because these types of verse, as patterns of sound, do not fit the acoustic and perceptual patterns of ordinary linguistic discourse. Only if we assume the discourse to have been a heightened one—something out of the ordinary, what I have been calling recitative—do three and four levels of metrical ictus make sense. And then they make sense readily, for the perceptual implications of an actual melody, a tune, pose no problems. I am assuming something like what George Herzog assumes for the music of Serbo-Croatian oral epic—that in examining words and music together, one may find "a structure which the poem as text does not have."[18]

In order for melody to be considered a structural element of Old English poetry, it is necessary that the relationship of words and music be exact, governed by rules much more rigorously than in Modern English song. Specifically, I would expect syllables with greater ictus to occur on notes of higher musical pitch. The musical pitch would then emphasize the appropriate syllables bearing ictus. Syllables with intermediate levels of ictus would occur on notes of intermediate pitch, syllables filling positions of non-ictus on lowest notes. Otherwise, if the melody failed to highlight the appropriate syllables or actually contradicted them, one is thrown back to the perceptual morass discussed above.

It is fair to ask whether such a model of words and music is at all plausible for Old English—whether anything like it has ever occurred. In fact, there is good reason to believe that much medieval music, religious and secular, was composed in accordance with rules similar to these. The origin of Latin neumes, by which Gregorian chant was notated, is a matter of some conjecture, but the most plausible hypothesis (and the one for which there is general consensus) derives the neumes from grammatical accent signs: the acute accent (´) indicated an elevation of the voice, the grave accent (`) a lowering. The various neumes—clivis, podatus, porrectus, etc.—are believed to have originally been combinations of the accent markings.[19] Whatever the origin of the notation, it is possible to deduce a clear relationship of grammatical accent and musical pitch from manuscripts of the ninth century and later. Paolo Ferretti, in his authoritative work on the subject, formulates a "law of accent," which states as a conclusion of his investigations essentially the same relationship of words and music that I have posited for Old English texts: syllables bearing ictus occur on higher notes of the melody, syllables bearing no ictus on lower notes, and syllables bearing intermediate ictus on notes of intermediate pitch.[20] Apel objects to Ferretti's description of his

observation as a "law," points out exceptions in addition to
exceptions that Ferretti himself lists, and asserts that the pitch
of the accented syllable should be compared only to syllables that
follow and not to those that precede.[21] Despite his objections to
details in the formulation, Apel grants that Ferretti's *loi de
l'accent* points toward "a very basic principle" of musical composition in the Middle Ages (p. 290). The point to make here is
that the melodic patterns posited above for Old English gain a
considerable amount of plausibility. From a purely theoretical
consideration of acoustic and perceptual matters, it was necessary
to propose certain constraints regarding words and music. I
originally formulated the constraints in ignorance of historical
example and was naturally pleased to discover that the historical
parallels not only exist, but also are remarkably close.[22]

It was also after formulating my own system for Old English that
I found I was not the first to do so—that Ewald Jammers had earlier
proposed similar correspondences between linguistic stress and
musical pitch for the older Germanic poetry.[23] Dietrich Hofmann,
following Jammers, proposes (and later rejects) musical settings
for four lines of Cædmon's Hymn:

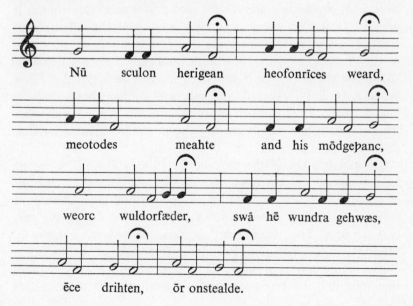

The absolute pitch is not of immediate concern, nor is the rhythm—only the relative pitch and the resulting contours. All of Hofmann's patterns correspond closely to those described here, except the D verse in the third line, which by my system would have a higher pitch on *weorc* than on *wul-*, instead of level pitch.[24]

For the opening lines of *Beowulf* I would expect similar melodic patterns. Since again it is the relative pitch instead of the absolute pitch that is our concern, a three-line staff will be appropriately noncommittal (see facing page).

I would take pains to emphasize that my conclusions regarding the Old English verse-form are hardly as novel as they may appear. Sixty years ago Kaluza asserted that the older poets "composed their verses merely by fitting the speech-material at their disposal to melodies of four members, which they received from an earlier time."[25] Through a rather different process of investigation, I arrived unexpectedly at Kaluza's conclusion. The abstract patterns of Chapter Seven require two mechanisms to give them perceptual and aesthetic reality: a correspondence of linguistic pitch and musical pitch within a style of recitative, and a principle of composition by melodic formula. The first mechanism, as we have seen, is plausible enough for medieval music, occurring as it does in Gregorian chant and elsewhere. And the principle of composition by melodic formula underlies not only the structure of the *chansons de geste* but more importantly the structure of Byzantine chant, where it has been studied at length by Egon Wellesz, H. J. W. Tillyard, and others.[26] Wellesz shows that the melodic formula was much more widespread in medieval times than originally believed, occurring also in Arabic, Syrian, Serbian, and Oriental music.

The possible use of the melodic formula in *Beowulf* brings us to a comment or two upon the various oral-formulaic theories of poetic composition in Old English poetry and the vast amount of scholarship that those theories have inspired during the past two decades. The seminal article was, of course, Francis P. Magoun, Jr.'s, "The Oral-Formulaic Character of Anglo-Saxon Narrative Poetry," *Speculum*, 28 (1953), 446–67. For the studies that followed, the best summary and evaluation is the excellent

HWÆT, WĒ GĀR–DEna   in gēardagum,

þēodcyninga   þrym gefrūnon,

hū ðā æþelingas   ellen fremedon!

Oft Scyld Scēfing   sceaþena þrēatum,

monegum mǣgþum   meodosetla oftēah,

egsode eorl[as],   syððan ǣrest wearð

fēasceaft funden;   hē þæs frōfre gebād,

wēox under wolcnum   weorðmyndum þāh,

oð þæt him ǣghwylc   ymbsittendra

ofer hronrāde   hȳran scolde,

gomban gyldan;   þæt wæs gōd cyning!

account by Ann Chalmers Watts, *The Lyre and the Harp: A Comparative Reconsideration of Oral Tradition in Homer and Old English* (New Haven: Yale University Press, 1969). Watts rightly points out that the transfer of Parry-Lord methodology from Homeric Greek to Old English was an imperfect transfer that paid too little attention to the metrical differences between the two literatures. In the search for syntactic and lexical repetitions, many studies assumed an inadequate definition of "formula" and often altogether ignored the underlying metrical constraints. Watts puts the emphasis where it belongs in defining a formula as "a repeated sequence that fills one of Sievers' five basic rhythmical types" (p. 90).

With this definition, the relationship between the lexical formula studied in Old English scholarship and the melodic formula studied in musicology becomes obvious. If lexical repetitions depend upon the underlying metrical structures, and if the metrical structures, such as the contours that I presented in Chapter Seven, can be understood as melodic formulas, then the problem becomes the traditional one of the relationship between words and melody. In Frederic G. Cassidy's "How Free Was the Anglo-Saxon Scop?" the priority of meter is twice acknowledged, but the emphasis is upon syntactic frames.[27] In Wellesz's chapter, "Words and Music," the emphasis is naturally upon linguistic stress and melodic pitch, with no attention paid to syntax.[28] If it is understood that each kind of study deals with a different aspect of the same problem, then a musicological study such as Wellesz's might well profit from considering syntactic frames such as those posited by Cassidy. And, from the other direction, an improvement might be made by substituting "melodic" for "rhythmical" in Watts's definition of formula to have it read, "a repeated sequence that fills one of Sievers' five basic *melodic* types." Pope has shown us that Sievers' five types are real at some level of description, but certainly not at the rhythmical level.

The matter of rhythm brings us finally to the lyre at Sutton Hoo.[29] The assumption of instrumental accompaniment is an important part of Pope's rhythmical theory, and his theory, in turn, has been cited with approval by Bessinger and Wrenn in their discussions of the Sutton Hoo instrument. Bessinger notes: "It was the rhythm of the harp, not its melody, which must have been useful and pleasing to the Old English singers, as to contemporary Slavic singers with their *gusle*."[30] While I find myself in general agreement with Pope, Bessinger, and Wrenn that the Old English poetic form was musical, as against Heusler and Lehmann,[31] I must reject, for reasons given in Chapter One, Pope's rhythmical theory and its assumption that the harp (or lyre) could repeatedly fill an incomplete linguistic structure. In this chapter I have given arguments for believing instead that the most important musical element was melody. If these arguments have any validity, then conclusions such as those reached by Bessinger, in his excellent studies of the musical background of Old English poetry, would require revision.

C. S. Lewis once wrote, in an instructive essay on prosody: "The first rule is 'Avoid the Inductive Method.'"[32] A paradigm of meter can "cover the facts" *too well* and fail for its very inclusiveness. The classification of Old English verses devised by Pope covers the facts: his 286 categories account for all of the lines in *Beowulf*. But the very complexity of the system prompted Creed to look for an underlying simplicity. And Bliss's 130 categories cause one to turn back to Sievers' system, from which the categories proliferated. If a simple system of meter can make the same *significant* distinctions that a more complex system makes, one should recognize two levels of adequacy and choose the descriptively adequate system over the one that merely accounts for the observed data. If one accepts the descriptively adequate system and is content with its logic but vaguely unhappy with its relation to the real world, then one must make an effort to explain what one has described.

Here I must confess my own bias and admit a certain satisfaction from working at the lowest level of description—searching out the various occurrences of *æþelinges* and trying to determine its pattern of stress. But the relationship of the stress on *æþelinges* to other patterns begins after a while to nag; the asymmetry of the various patterns makes its own discomfort; and the import of

Lewis's warning against proceeding inductively becomes clear. One then considers the separate problems together and discovers that indeed they have a logical relationship. But that is not all. If the Old English verse-form has its own logic, it also has an aesthetic reality that the poet and his audience perceived. In translating the abstract pattern of meter into the related patterns of linguistic and musical pitch, I have tried to ask appropriate questions about that perceived reality so that adequate answers may eventually be given. Then we may be able to recapture something of a lost mode of perception and understand better an unfamiliar form of poetry.

NOTES

1 See George L. Trager and Henry Lee Smith, Jr., *An Outline of English Structure*, Studies in Linguistics: Occasional Papers, 3 (1951; rpt. Washington: American Council of Learned Societies, 1957), pp. 35–39.

2 See James Sledd, rev. of Trager and Smith, *Outline*, in *Language*, 31 (1955), 324; see also Philip Lieberman, "On the Acoustic Basis of the Perception of Intonation by Linguists," *Word*, 21 (1965), 40–54; and, for Swedish, Kerstin Hadding-Koch, *Acoustico-Phonetic Studies in the Intonation of Southern Swedish*, Travaux de l'Institut de Phonétique de Lund, 3 (Lund: Gleerup, 1961), p. 50.

3 See Philip Lieberman, *Intonation, Perception, and Language*, Research Monograph, No. 38 (Cambridge, Mass.: MIT Press, 1967), pp. 144–47.

4 See also D. B. Fry, "Experiments in the Perception of Stress," *Language and Speech*, 1 (1958), 126–29; Dwight L. Bolinger, "A Theory of Pitch Accent in English," *Word*, 14 (1958), 111–13; and David Crystal, *Prosodic Systems and Intonation in English*, Cambridge Studies in Linguistics, 1 (Cambridge: Cambridge University Press, 1969), pp. 108–21.

5 Noam Chomsky and Morris Halle, *The Sound Pattern of English* (New York: Harper and Row, 1968), p. 23.

6 A view, as Lieberman points out, quite similar to that held by Daniel Jones, *An Outline of English Phonetics*, 9th ed. (Cambridge: Heffer, 1962), p. 245*n*.

7 See Lieberman, *Intonation*, pp. 147–48; see also D. B. Fry, "Duration and Intensity as Physical Correlates of Linguistic Stress," *Journal of the Acoustical Society of America*, 27 (1955), 765–68.

8 Lieberman, *Intonation*, pp. 148–49.

9 Otto Jespersen, "Notes on Metre," in *Linguistica: Selected Papers in English, French and German* (Copenhagen: Levin and Munksgaard, 1933), p. 259.

10 W. K. Wimsatt, Jr., and Monroe C. Beardsley, "The Concept of Meter: An Exercise in Abstraction," *PMLA*, 74 (1959), 593.

11 See B. Q. Morgan, "Zur Lehre von der Alliteration in der westgermanischen Dichtung," *Beiträge zur Geschichte der deutschen Sprache und Literatur*, 33 (1908), 95–181; Sievers, *Rhythmisch-Melodische Studien: Vorträge und Aufsätze* (Heidelberg: Winter, 1912); Sievers, "Ziele und Wege der Schallanalyse," in *Stand und Aufgaben der Sprachwissenschaft: Festschrift für Wilhelm Streitberg*, ed. J. Friedrich et al. (Heidelberg: Winter, 1924), pp. 65–111; Sievers, "Zu Cynewulf," in *Neusprachliche*

Studien, Festgabe Karl Luick (*Die Neueren Sprachen*, 6 sup., 1925), pp. 60–81; Henry G. Atkins, *A History of German Versification: Ten Centuries of Metrical Evolution* (London: Methuen, 1923), pp. 32–36; and Gunther Ipsen and Fritz Karg, *Schallanalytische Versuche: Eine Einführung in die Schallanalyse* (Heidelberg: Winter, 1928).

12 Willi Apel, *Harvard Dictionary of Music*, 2nd ed. rev. (Cambridge, Mass.: Harvard University Press, 1969), p. 718.

13 J. Smits van Waesberghe, "Phonetics in Its Relation to Musicology," in *Manual of Phonetics*, ed. L. Kaiser (Amsterdam: North-Holland Publishing Co., 1957), pp. 372–84.

14 Ibid., p. 381. See also Walter Salmen, "European Song (1300–1530)," in *New Oxford History of Music*, ed. J. A. Westrup et al., rev. ed. (London: Oxford University Press, 1955), III, 357: "Everywhere, whether in Hungary or in Lithuania, in Germany or in Portugal, the old heroic epics, the *cantares de gesta* sung by *juglares épicos* to short verse-melodies, were all declining at this time, and the folk ballad and romance were being partially transformed or substantially remoulded into the style in which the political song was sung."

15 See Johannes Wolf, "Die Musiklehre des Johannes de Grocheo," *Sammelbände der internationalen Musikgesellschaft*, 1 (1899–1900), 94: "Idem etiam cantus debet in omnibus versibus reiterari."

16 J. A. Westrup, "Medieval Song," in *New Oxford History of Music*, II, 223.

17 See Friedrich Gennrich, *Der musikalische Vortrag der altfranzösischen Chansons de geste* (Halle: Niemeyer, 1923); and *Grundriss einer Formenlehre des mittelalterlichen Liedes als Grundlage einer musikalischen Formenlehre des Liedes* (Halle: Niemeyer, 1932).

18 George Herzog, "The Music of Yugoslav Heroic Epic Folk Poetry," *Journal of the International Folk Music Council*, 3 (1951), 63.

19 See Gustave Reese, *Music in the Middle Ages* (New York: Norton, 1940), pp. 132–33.

20 Paolo Ferretti, *Esthétique grégorienne*, trans. A. Agaësse (Tournai, Belgium: Desclée & Cie., 1938), p. 7: "Cette syllabe privilégiée [the most heavily stressed of the word] était mise en relief par un ton de voix plus *aigu*, plus *élevé* pendant que les autres syllabes, ses sujettes, étaient proférées d'un ton *bas, grave* et aussi—dans le cas de polysyllabes—d'un ton *moyen* entre le grave et l'aigu. De cette succession et alternance de tons aigus, graves et moyens naissait un *chant*, une *mélodie*, naturel, simple, embryonnaire."

21 Willi Apel, *Gregorian Chant* (Bloomington: Indiana University Press, 1966), pp. 289–97.

22 For further possible parallels, in Greek hymns of the second century B.C., see J. F. Mountford, "Greek Music in the Papyri and Inscriptions," in *New Chapters in the History of Greek Literature*, 2nd ser., ed. J. U. Powell and E. A. Barber (Oxford: Clarendon Press, 1929), pp. 146–83; S. Eitrem, Leiv Amundsen, and R. P. Winnington-Ingram, "Fragments of Unknown Greek Tragic Texts with Musical Notation," *Symbolae Osloenses*, 31 (1955), 57, 64–73; and R. P. Winnington-Ingram, "Ancient Greek Music: 1932–1957," *Lustrum*, 3 (1958), 5–57. For non-Indo-European parallels, see George Herzog, "Speech-Melody and Primitive Music," *Musical Quarterly*, 20 (1934), 452–66; Bruno Nettl, "Text-Music Relations in Arapaho Songs," *Southwestern Journal of Anthropology*, 10 (1954), 192–99; and Hans-Heinrich Wängler,

"Singen und Sprechen in einer Tonsprache (Hausa)," *Zeitschrift für Phonetik und allgemeine Sprachwissenschaft,* 11 (1958), 23–34.

23 See Ewald Jammers, "Das mittelalterliche deutsche Epos und die Musik," *Heidelberger Jahrbücher,* 1 (1957), 50, 89.

24 Dietrich Hofmann, "Die Frage des musikalischen Vortrags der altgermanischen Stabreimdichtung in philologischer Sicht," *Zeitschrift für deutsches Alterum und deutsche Literatur,* 92 (1963), 101; see also Karl H. Bertau and Rudolf Stephan, rev. of Jammers, "Das mittelalterliche," *Anzeiger für deutsches Alterum und deutsche Literatur,* 71 (1958), 57–74; Ewald Jammers, "Der Vortrag des altgermanischen Stabreimverses in musikwissenschaftlicher Sicht," *Zeitschrift für deutsches Alterum und deutsche Literatur,* 93 (1964), 1–13; and Dietrich Hofmann and Ewald Jammers, "Zur Frage des Vortrags der altgermanischen Stabreimdichtung," *Zeitschrift für deutsches Alterum und deutsche Literatur,* 94 (1965), 185–95.

25 Max Kaluza, *A Short History of English Versification,* trans. A. C. Dunstan (London: Allen, 1911), p. 74.

26 See H. J. W. Tillyard, *Handbook of the Middle Byzantine Musical Notation,* Monumenta Musicae Byzantinae, Subsidia, I, fasc. 1 (Copenhagen: Levin and Munksgaard, 1935); Egon Wellesz, *Eastern Elements in Western Chant,* Monumenta Musicae Byzantinae, Subsidia, II (Oxford: Oxford University Press, 1947); Miloš M. Velimirović, *Byzantine Elements in Early Slavic Chant: The Hirmologion,* Monumenta Musicae Byzantinae, Subsidia, IV (Copenhagen: Munksgaard, 1960); and Egon Wellesz, *A History of Byzantine Music and Hymnography,* 2nd ed. rev. (Oxford: Clarendon Press, 1961).

27 Frederic G. Cassidy, "How Free Was the Anglo-Saxon Scop?" in *Franciplegius: Medieval and Linguistic Studies in Honor of Francis Peabody Magoun, Jr.,* ed. Jess B. Bessinger, Jr., and Robert P. Creed (New York: New York University Press, 1965), pp. 77–78, 83.

28 Wellesz, *A History,* pp. 349–62.

29 The instrument was reconstructed in 1948 as a small rectangular harp, but recent evidence suggests that it is a larger Germanic "round lyre," about 29 inches long. See Rupert Bruce-Mitford, *The Sutton Hoo Ship-Burial: A Handbook,* 2nd ed. (London: British Museum, 1972), pp. 28–29.

30 Jess B. Bessinger, Jr., "*Beowulf* and the Harp at Sutton Hoo," *UTQ,* 27 (1958), 160; see also Bessinger, "The Sutton Hoo Harp Replica and Old English Musical Verse," in *Old English Poetry: Fifteen Essays,* ed. Robert P. Creed (Providence, R.I.: Brown University Press, 1967), pp. 15–16; C. L. Wrenn, "Sutton Hoo and *Beowulf,*" in *Mélanges de linguistique et de philologie, Fernand Mossé in Memoriam* (Paris: Didier, 1959), p. 502; and Wrenn, "Two Anglo-Saxon Harps," *Comparative Literature,* 14 (1962), 118.

31 See Andreas Heusler, *Die altgermanische Dichtung* (Berlin: Akademische Verlagsgesellschaft Athenaion, 1923), pp. 36–39; *Deutsche Versgeschichte mit Einschluss des altenglischen und altnordischen Stabreimverses,* Paul's *Grundriss der germanischen Philologie,* 8.1 (Berlin: Gruyter, 1925), pp. 90–91; and Winfred P. Lehmann, *The Development of Germanic Verse Form* (Austin: University of Texas Press and Linguistic Society of America, 1956), pp. 128–31.

32 C. S. Lewis, "Metre," *Review of English Literature,* 1, No. 1 (1960), 47.

Bibliography

Amelung, Arthur. "Beiträge zur deutschen Metrik," *Zeitschrift für deutsche Philologie*, 3 (1871), 253–305.

Apel, Willi. *Gregorian Chant*. Bloomington: Indiana University Press, 1966.

———. *Harvard Dictionary of Music*. 2nd ed. rev. Cambridge, Mass.: Harvard University Press, 1969.

Atkins, Henry G. *A History of German Versification: Ten Centuries of Metrical Evolution*. London: Methuen, 1923.

Baum, Paull F. "The Character of Anglo-Saxon Verse," *MP*, 28 (1930), 143–56.

———. "The Meter of the *Beowulf*," *MP*, 46 (1948–49), 73–91, 145–62.

Bertau, Karl H., and Rudolf Stephan. Review of "Das mittelalterliche deutsche Epos und die Musik," by E. Jammers. *Anzeiger für deutsches Alterum und deutsche Literatur*, 71 (1958), 57–74.

Bessinger, Jess B., Jr. "*Beowulf* and the Harp at Sutton Hoo," *UTQ*, 27 (1958), 148–68.

———. *Beowulf, Caedmon's Hymn and Other Old English Poems*. New York: Caedmon Records, Inc., 1962.

———. "The Sutton Hoo Harp Replica and Old English Musical Verse." *Old English Poetry: Fifteen Essays*. Ed. Robert P. Creed. Providence, R.I.: Brown University Press, 1967, pp. 3–26.

Bliss, A. J. "The Appreciation of Old English Metre." *English and Medieval Studies Presented to J. R. R. Tolkien on the Occasion of his Seventieth Birthday*. Ed. Norman Davis and C. L. Wrenn. London: Allen and Unwin, 1962, pp. 27–40.

————. *The Metre of Beowulf.* 2nd ed. rev. Oxford: Blackwell, 1967.

Bolinger, Dwight L. "A Theory of Pitch Accent in English," *Word*, 14 (1958), 109–49.

Bruce-Mitford, Rupert. *The Sutton Hoo Ship-Burial: A Handbook.* 2nd ed. London: British Museum, 1972.

Cable, Thomas. "Rules for Syntax and Metrics in *Beowulf*," *JEGP*, 69 (1970), 81–88.

————. "Timers, Stressers, and Linguists: Contention and Compromise," *MLQ*, 33 (1972), 227–39.

Campbell, A[listair]. *Old English Grammar.* Rev. ed. Oxford: Clarendon Press, 1962.

Cassidy, Frederic G. "How Free Was the Anglo-Saxon Scop?" *Franciplegius: Medieval and Linguistic Studies in Honor of Francis Peabody Magoun, Jr.* Ed. Jess B. Bessinger, Jr., and Robert P. Creed. New York: New York University Press, 1965, pp. 75–85.

Chomsky, Noam. "Current Issues in Linguistic Theory." *The Structure of Language: Readings in the Philosophy of Language.* Ed. Jerry A. Fodor and Jerrold J. Katz. Englewood Cliffs, N.J.: Prentice-Hall, 1964, pp. 50–118.

————, and Morris Halle. *The Sound Pattern of English.* New York: Harper and Row, 1968.

Clemoes, Peter. *Liturgical Influence on Punctuation in Late Old English and Early Middle English Manuscripts.* Occasional Papers, No. 1. Cambridge: Department of Anglo-Saxon, 1952.

Clemons, Elinor D. "A Metrical Analysis of the Old English Poem *Exodus.*" Ph.D. dissertation, University of Texas, 1961.

Cooper, Grosvenor W., and Leonard B. Meyer. *The Rhythmic Structure of Music.* Chicago: University of Chicago Press, 1960.

Creed, Robert P. "A New Approach to the Rhythm of *Beowulf*," *PMLA*, 81 (1966), 23–33.

Crystal, David. *Prosodic Systems and Intonation in English.* Cambridge Studies in Linguistics, 1. Cambridge: Cambridge University Press, 1969.

Daunt, Marjorie. "Old English Verse and English Speech Rhythm," *Transactions of the Philological Society* (1946), pp. 56–72.

Eitrem, S., Leiv Amundsen, and R. P. Winnington-Ingram. "Fragments of Unknown Greek Tragic Texts with Musical Notation," *Symbolae Osloenses*, 31 (1955), 1–87.

Ferretti, Paolo. *Esthétique grégorienne.* Trans. A. Agaësse. Tournai, Belgium: Desclée & Cie., 1938.

Fry, D. B. "Duration and Intensity as Physical Correlates of Linguistic Stress," *Journal of the Acoustical Society of America*, 27 (1955), 765–68.

———. "Experiments in the Perception of Stress," *Language and Speech*, 1 (1958), 126–52.

Frye, Northrop. *Anatomy of Criticism: Four Essays*. 1957; rpt. New York: Atheneum, 1966.

Gennrich, Friedrich. *Der musikalische Vortrag der altfranzösischen Chansons de geste*. Halle: Niemeyer, 1923.

———. *Grundriss einer Formenlehre des mittelalterlichen Liedes als Grundlage einer musikalischen Formenlehre des Liedes*. Halle: Niemeyer, 1932.

Girvan, Ritchie. Review of *The Rhythm of Beowulf*, by John C. Pope. *RES*, 19 (1943), 73–77.

Greg, W. W. "The 'Five Types' in Anglo-Saxon Verse," *Modern Language Review*, 20 (1925), 12–17.

Hadding-Koch, Kerstin. *Acoustico-Phonetic Studies in the Intonation of Southern Swedish*. Travaux de l'Institut de Phonétique de Lund, 3. Lund: Gleerup, 1961.

Hall, John R. Clark, trans. *Beowulf and the Finnesburg Fragment*. 3rd ed. rev. C. L. Wrenn. "Prefatory Remarks" by J. R. R. Tolkien. London: Allen and Unwin, 1950.

Halle, Morris, and Samuel Jay Keyser. "Chaucer and the Study of Prosody," *College English*, 28 (1966), 187–219.

Herzog, George. "Speech-Melody and Primitive Music," *Musical Quarterly*, 20 (1934), 452–66.

———. "The Music of Yugoslav Heroic Epic Folk Poetry," *Journal of the International Folk Music Council*, 3 (1951), 62–64.

Heusler, Andreas. *Die altgermanische Dichtung*. Berlin: Akademische Verlagsgesellschaft Athenaion, 1923.

———. *Deutsche Versgeschichte mit Einschluss des altenglischen und altnordischen Stabreimverses*. Paul's *Grundriss der germanischen Philologie*, 8.1. Berlin: Gruyter, 1925.

Hofmann, Dietrich. "Die Frage des musikalischen Vortrags der altgermanischen Stabreimdichtung in philologischer Sicht," *Zeitschrift für deutsches Alterum und deutsche Literatur*, 92 (1963), 83–121.

———, and Ewald Jammers. "Zur Frage des Vortrags der altgermanischen Stabreimdichtung," *Zeitschrift für deutsches Alterum und deutsche Literatur*, 94 (1965), 185–95.

Ipsen, Gunther, and Fritz Karg. *Schallanalytische Versuche: Eine*

Einführung in die Schallanalyse. Heidelberg: Winter, 1928.

Jammers, Ewald. "Das mittelalterliche deutsche Epos und die Musik," *Heidelberger Jahrbücher,* 1 (1957), 31–90.

———. "Der Vortrag des altgermanischen Stabriemverses in musikwissenschaftlicher Sicht," *Zeitschrift für deutsches Alterum und deutsche Literatur,* 93 (1964), 1–13.

Jespersen, Otto. "Notes on Metre." *Linguistica: Selected Papers in English, French and German.* Copenhagen: Levin and Munksgaard, 1933, pp. 249–74.

Jessen, E. "Grundzüge der altgermanischen Metrik," *Zeitschrift für deutsche Philologie,* 2 (1870), 114–47.

Jones, Daniel. *An Outline of English Phonetics.* 9th ed. Cambridge: Heffer, 1962.

Kaluza, Max. *Englische Metrik in historischer Entwicklung dargestellt.* Berlin: Felber, 1909.

———. *A Short History of English Versification from the Earliest Times to the Present Day.* Trans. A. C. Dunstan. London: Allen, 1911.

Keyser, Samuel Jay. "Old English Prosody," *College English,* 30 (1969), 331–56.

Klaeber, Fr., ed. *Beowulf and the Fight at Finnsburg.* 3rd ed. Boston: Heath, 1950.

Kuhn, Thomas S. *The Structure of Scientific Revolutions.* Chicago: University of Chicago Press, 1962.

Lachmann, Karl. "Über althochdeutsche Betonung und Verskunst" and "Über das Hildebrandslied." *Kleinere Schriften zur deutschen Philologie.* Ed. Karl Müllenhoff. Vol. 1 of *Kleinere Schriften von Karl Lachmann.* Berlin: Reimer, 1876, pp. 358–406, 407–48.

Lehmann, Winfred P. *The Development of Germanic Verse Form.* Austin: University of Texas Press and Linguistic Society of America, 1956.

———. "Metrical Evidence for Old English Suprasegmentals," *Texas Studies in Literature and Language,* 1 (1959), 66–72.

———. Review of *The Metre of Beowulf,* by A. J. Bliss. *JEGP,* 59 (1960), 137–42.

Le Page, R. B. "A Rhythmical Framework for the Five Types," *English and Germanic Studies,* 6 (1957), 92–103.

Lewis, C. S. "Metre," *Review of English Literature,* 1, No. 1 (1960), 45–50.

Lieberman, Philip. "On the Acoustic Basis of the Perception of Intonation by Linguists," *Word,* 21 (1965), 40–54.

————. *Intonation, Perception, and Language*. Research Monograph No. 38. Cambridge, Mass.: MIT Press, 1967.

McIntosh, Angus. "Wulfstan's Prose," *Proceedings of the British Academy*, 35 (1949), 109–42.

Magoun, Francis, P., Jr. "The Oral-Formulaic Character of Anglo-Saxon Narrative Poetry," *Speculum*, 28 (1953), 446–67.

Malof, Joseph. "The Native Rhythm of English Meters," *Texas Studies in Literature and Language*, 5 (1964), 580–94.

Morgan, B. Q. "Zur Lehre von der Alliteration in der westgermanischen Dichtung," *Beiträge zur Geschichte der deutschen Sprache und Literatur*, 33 (1908), 95–181.

Mountford, J. F. "Greek Music in the Papyri and Inscriptions." *New Chapters in the History of Greek Literature*, 2nd ser. Ed. J. U. Powell and E. A. Barber. Oxford: Clarendon Press, 1929, pp. 146–83.

Nettl, Bruno. "Text-Music Relations in Arapaho Songs," *Southwestern Journal of Anthropology*, 10 (1954), 192–99.

Nist, John. "Metrical Uses of the Harp in *Beowulf*." *Old English Poetry: Fifteen Essays*. Ed. Robert P. Creed. Providence, R.I.: Brown University Press, 1967, pp. 27–43.

Oakden, J. P. *Alliterative Poetry in Middle English*. 1930–35; rpt. [Hamden, Conn.] Archon, 1968.

Pope, John C. *The Rhythm of Beowulf: An Interpretation of the Normal and Hypermetric Verse-Forms in Old English Poetry*. 2nd ed. rev. New Haven: Yale University Press, 1966.

————, ed. *Seven Old English Poems*. New York: Bobbs-Merrill, 1966.

————. *Selections from Beowulf*. Pleasantville, N.Y.: Educational Audio Visual, Inc.

Reese, Gustave. *Music in the Middle Ages: With an Introduction on the Music of Ancient Times*. New York: Norton, 1940.

Salmen, Walter. "European Song (1300–1530)." *New Oxford History of Music*. Ed. J. A. Westrup et al. Rev. ed. London: Oxford University Press, 1955. III, 349–80.

Schipper, Jakob. *A History of English Versification*. Oxford: Clarendon Press, 1910.

Sedgefield, W. J. *An Anglo-Saxon Book of Verse and Prose*. Publications of the University of Manchester, 186, English Series, 17. Manchester: Manchester University Press, 1928.

Sievers, Eduard. "Zur Rhythmik des germanischen Alliterationsverses I," *Beiträge zur Geschichte der deutschen Sprache und Literatur*, 10 (1885), 209–314.

————. *Altgermanische Metrik*. Halle: Niemeyer, 1893.

————. *Rhythmisch-Melodische Studien: Vorträge und Aufsätze*. Heidelberg: Winter, 1912.

————. "Ziele und Wege der Schallanalyse." *Stand und Aufgaben der Sprachwissenschaft: Festschrift für Wilhelm Streitberg*. Ed. J. Friedrich et al. Heidelberg: Winter, 1924, pp. 65–111.

————. "Zu Cynewulf." *Neusprachliche Studien, Festgabe Karl Luick* (*Die Neueren Sprachen*, 6 sup., 1925), pp. 60–81.

Sir Gawain and the Green Knight. Ed. J. R. R. Tolkien and E. V. Gordon. 2nd ed. rev. Norman Davis. Oxford: Clarendon Press, 1968.

Sledd, James. Review of *An Outline of English Structure*, by G. L. Trager and H. L. Smith, Jr. *Language*, 31 (1955), 312–45.

————. "Old English Prosody: A Demurrer," *College English*, 31 (1969), 71–74.

Smits van Waesberghe, J. "Phonetics in Its Relation to Musicology." *Manual of Phonetics*. Ed. L. Kaiser. Amsterdam: North-Holland Publishing Co., 1957, pp. 372–84.

Stevick, Robert D. *English and Its History: The Evolution of a Language*. Boston: Allyn and Bacon, 1968.

————. *Suprasegmentals, Meter, and the Manuscript of Beowulf*. The Hague: Mouton, 1968.

Stewart, George R., Jr. *The Technique of English Verse*. New York: Holt, 1930.

Sweet, Henry. *A New English Grammar, Logical and Historical*. Vol. 1. Oxford: Clarendon Press, 1900.

————. *An Anglo-Saxon Reader in Prose and Verse*. 9th ed. rev. C. T. Onions. Oxford: Clarendon Press, 1922.

Taglicht, Josef. "*Beowulf* and Old English Verse Rhythm," *RES*, n.s. 12 (1961), 341–51.

ten Brink, Bernhard. "Altenglische Literatur." *Grundriss der germanischen Philologie*. Ed. Hermann Paul. II, pt. 1. Strassburg: Trübner, 1893, 510–50.

Tillyard, H. J. W. *Handbook of the Middle Byzantine Musical Notation*. Monumenta Musicae Byzantinae, Subsidia, I, fasc. 1. Copenhagen: Levin and Munksgaard, 1935.

Trager, George L., and Henry Lee Smith, Jr. *An Outline of English Structure*. Studies in Linguistics: Occasional Papers, 3. 1951; rpt. Washington: American Council of Learned Societies, 1957.

Trautmann, Moritz. "Die neueste Beowulfausgabe und die altenglische Verslehre," *Bonner Beiträge zur Anglistik*, 17 (1905), 175–91.

Velimirović, Miloš, M. *Byzantine Elements in Early Slavic Chant: The Hirmologion.* Monumenta Musicae Byzantinae, Subsidia, IV. Copenhagen: Munksgaard, 1960.

Wängler, Hans-Heinrich. "Singen und Sprechen in einer Tonsprache (Hausa)," *Zeitschrift für Phonetik und allegemeine Sprachwissenschaft,* 11 (1958), 23–34.

Watts, Ann Chalmers. *The Lyre and the Harp: A Comparative Reconsideration of Oral Tradition in Homer and Old English Epic Poetry.* New Haven: Yale University Press, 1969.

Wellesz, Egon. *Eastern Elements in Western Chant: Studies in the Early History of Ecclesiastical Music.* Monumenta Musicae Byzantinae, Subsidia, II. Oxford: Oxford University Press, 1947.

———. *A History of Byzantine Music and Hymnography.* 2nd ed. rev. Oxford: Clarendon Press, 1961.

Westrup, J. A. "Medieval Song." *New Oxford History of Music.* Ed. J. A. Westrup et al. Rev. ed. London: Oxford University Press, 1955. II, 220–69.

Willard, Rudolph, and Elinor D. Clemons. "Bliss's Light Verses in the *Beowulf,*" *JEGP,* 66 (1967), 230–44.

Wimsatt, W. K., Jr., and Monroe C. Beardsley. "The Concept of Meter: An Exercise in Abstraction," *PMLA,* 74 (1959), 585–98.

Winnington-Ingram, R. P. "Ancient Greek Music: 1932–1957," *Lustrum,* 3 (1958), 5–57.

Wolf, Johannes. "Die Musiklehre des Johannes de Grocheo: Ein Beitrag zur Musikgeschichte des Mittelalters," *Sammelbände der internationalen Musikgesellschaft,* 1 (1899–1900), 65–130.

Wrenn, C. L. "On the Continuity of English Poetry," *Anglia,* 76 (1958), 41–59.

———. "Sutton Hoo and *Beowulf.*" *Mélanges de linguistique et de philologie, Fernand Mossé in Memoriam.* Paris: Didier, 1959, pp. 495–507.

———. "Two Anglo-Saxon Harps," *Comparative Literature,* 14 (1962), 118–28.

Wyatt, A. J., and R. W. Chambers, eds. *Beowulf with the Finnsburg Fragment.* 1914; rpt. Cambridge: Cambridge University Press, 1952.

Index